STATE AND UNCIVIL
SOCIETY IN THAILAND
AT THE TEMPLE OF
PREAH VIHEAR

The **Institute of Southeast Asian Studies** (**ISEAS**) was established as an autonomous organization in 1968. It is a regional centre dedicated to the study of socio-political, security and economic trends and developments in Southeast Asia and its wider geostrategic and economic environment. The Institute's research programmes are the Regional Economic Studies (RES, including ASEAN and APEC), Regional Strategic and Political Studies (RSPS), and Regional Social and Cultural Studies (RSCS).

ISEAS Publishing, an established academic press, has issued more than 2,000 books and journals. It is the largest scholarly publisher of research about Southeast Asia from within the region. ISEAS Publishing works with many other academic and trade publishers and distributors to disseminate important research and analyses from and about Southeast Asia to the rest of the world.

STATE AND UNCIVIL SOCIETY IN THAILAND AT THE TEMPLE OF PREAH VIHEAR

PUANGTHONG R. PAWAKAPAN

LSEAS

INSTITUTE OF SOUTHEAST ASIAN STUDIES

Singapore

First published in Singapore in 2013 by
ISEAS Publishing
Institute of Southeast Asian Studies
30 Heng Mui Keng Terrace
Pasir Panjang
Singapore 119614
E-mail: publish@iseas.edu.sg
Website: http://bookshop.iseas.edu.sg

The responsibility for facts and opinions in this publication rests exclusively with the author and her interpretations do not necessarily reflect the views or the policy of the Institute or its supports.

ISEAS Library Cataloguing-in-Publication Data

Puangthong R. Pawakapan.
   State and uncivil society in Thailand at the Temple of Preah Vihear.
   1. Prasat Prĕah Vihéar (Cambodia)—International status.
   2. Prasat Prĕah Vihéar (Cambodia)—Claims vs. Cambodia.
   3. Thailand—Foreign relations—Cambodia.
   4. Cambodia—Foreign relations—Thailand.
   5. Civil society—Thailand.
   6. Thailand—Politics and government—1988–
   I. Title
DS575.5 C15P97   2013

ISBN 978-981-4459-90-7 (soft cover)
ISBN 978-981-4459-91-4 (E-book PDF)

Cover photo: Reproduced with kind permission from Sukum Cheewakiatyingyong.

Typeset by Superskill Graphics Pte Ltd
Printed in Singapore by Mainland Press Pte Ltd

For all my teachers:
Chaiwat Satha-anand, Charnvit Kasetsiri,
Ben Kiernan, Adrian Vickers, the late Melanie Beresford,
and Thawit Sukhapanich

Contents

List of Tables

List of Pictures

Preface

This study examines the role of Thai state agencies and the mass movement led by the People's Alliance for Democracy (PAD) in the dispute over the Preah Vihear temple located close to the Thai-Cambodian border. It also evaluates the long-term repercussions of the PAD's uncivil action within the context of Thailand's post-Cold War policy towards its neighbours in general and Cambodia in particular.

The ending of the Cold War and of the war in Cambodia in the late 1980s opened up opportunities for a new era of economic development and cooperation in Southeast Asia. Thailand positioned herself as a centre of economic cooperation in the region. Policies promoted by various state agencies reshaped the relationship between Thailand and Cambodia from enmity to economic interdependence. Thailand's support for Cambodia's proposal to list the Preah Vihear temple as a World Heritage site arose from Thailand's cross-border tourism strategy.

The relationship between Thailand and Cambodia deteriorated greatly in mid-2008 when the PAD raised a protest against the proposed listing, claiming that it was linked to business deals by the former Thai prime minister Thaksin Shinawatra in Cambodia, and that it would sacrifice Thai ownership of a disputed area around the temple.

However, the PAD's allegation overlooks the fact that the bilateral cooperation over the listing was pursued consistently by three Thai governments and various bureaucratic agencies in an attempt to turn the once disputed monument into a symbol of friendship and cooperation between the two countries. For the first time in Southeast Asia two formerly antagonistic states were employing economic and cultural methods to settle a territorial dispute.

The ultra-nationalist movement launched by PAD not only derailed this essay in cooperation but also worked directly against Thailand's post-Cold

War strategy in the region. Instead of becoming a symbol of friendship, the temple became a symbol of hatred between Thailand and Cambodia. The success of the PAD's campaign is due in part to the support which PAD received from various civic groups and institutions. This support helped to legitimize the PAD's lies and propaganda, which shaped the Thai public's misperception of the issue. The role of the PAD challenges the conventional wisdom that active civil society movements contribute to democratization.

The primary objective of this study is thus to analyse the actions, strategy, and objectives of the PAD campaign on the Preah Vihear temple and the disputed area surrounding the temple. It will focus on factors enabling the PAD to successfully mobilize widespread support for its campaign. The study also evaluates the impact of the PAD movement on Thai-Cambodian relations and on the perceptions of Thai foreign policy decision-makers, including political leaders, the Foreign Affairs Ministry, and the military.

First it is imperative to understand the relationship between Thailand and Cambodia in the post-Cold War era, prior to the PAD campaign. I argue that expanding economic ties have shaped a bilateral relationship based on interdependence rather than enmity. This interdependence influenced the perceptions and practices of Thai foreign policy-makers. The study starts in this post-Cold War era of growing interdependence and ends at the close of the government of Abhisit Vejjajiva in July 2011.

The following chapters fall into four sections. The first chapter sets the stage, providing an overall picture of how the conflict between Thailand and Cambodia over the temple of Preah Vihear began and of various actors involved in the saga. It also discusses conceptual framework of complex interdependence and uncivil society used in this work. Chapter II discusses the change of Thailand's foreign policy toward its neighbours in the post-Cold War period as background for understanding the broad context within which the Thai and Cambodian governments entered into cooperation over the temple. Chapter III traces the development of bilateral cooperation up to the agreement to jointly promote the listing of the temple as a World Heritage site. Chapter IV examines the nature of the PAD, the objectives and tactics of its campaign over the temple, and its impact on the government, foreign policy-making, and international relations.

Acknowledgements

The book was an outcome of my research fellowship at the Walter H. Shorenstein Asia Pacific Research Center, Stanford University, between August 2010 and June 2011. The fellowship was sponsored by the Asia Foundation. It would not have been achieved without kindness and support from several people and organizations. First and foremost is Professor Chaiwat Satha-anand, who nominated me as a candidate for the Shorenstein APARC/Asia Foundation Fellowship. I am greatly indebt to the constant caring and support Chaiwat has had for me since I was his student at Thammasat University.

Professor Charnvit Kasetsiri was an inspiration for me to seriously take up the issue of the temple of Preah Vihear. His courage to fight against nationalist blindness in Thai society is indeed admirable. Despite nasty attacks from the ultra-nationalists, he bravely stands up to them.

I am very grateful to the Asia Foundation for granting me the fellowship. My special thanks also go to Dr Vera Young and Nadia Kelly of the San Francisco office for their kind and generous support in many ways during my ten-month stay in Palo Alto. Poonsook Pantitanonta of the Bangkok office kindly assisted me with all the necessities before I left for California. Denise Masumoto and Lisa Lee of APARC were very kind and helpful to me and made my time at Stanford an enjoyable year. It was such a great opportunity for me to have a peaceful time in a beautiful town of Palo Alto and to be able to turn my thoughts into a research paper — something I would not have been able to achieve in a hectic life with the never-ending political crisis in Thailand. A richly academic environment at Stanford was an intellectual refreshment for me. Besides, the fellowship allowed my eleven-year-old son, Pian, an exciting educational experience at the Jane Latrop Stanford Middle School. Thanks to my husband, Niti Pawakapan, for his constant support for me to take up the fellowship.

My sincere thanks also to the Institute of Southeast Asian Studies, Singapore, for publishing my work and to the ISEAS Publishing staff for taking care of this book project. My appreciation also goes to my colleagues at the Department of International Relations, Faculty of Political Science, for their moral support, and to Supamit Patipat in particular for providing the Department funding to cover extra costs for this book project. I truly appreciate comments and suggestions from Don Emmerson, the two anonymous readers, and Supamit Pitipat. Last but not least, Chris Baker carefully read and edited the manuscript for me. His editing skills and critical comments helped improve the quality of the book. His kindness and generosity truly impressed me.

CHAPTER I

Introduction

During the Cold War, when military security was a top priority, decision making on foreign policy in Thailand was a simple process with a state-centric character. It mainly involved a number of key state agencies, including the military high command, National Security Council, Ministry of Foreign Affairs, and government leaders. After the Cold War ended, former communist countries were welcomed into the once anti-communist regional grouping of ASEAN. The Thai state agencies appeared capable of handling the post-Cold War relationship with their former enemies fairly smoothly. Though there was a hiccup in 2003, when an angry Cambodian mob burned down the Thai embassy and business buildings in Phnom Penh after a Thai actress had allegedly said that Angkor Wat belonged to Thailand, the crisis ended quickly and a normal relationship was resumed soon after. Thai-Cambodian relations, however, spiralled downwards when a civil society movement in Thailand raised a campaign over the temple of Preah Vihear which is situated on the border between the two countries. The movement was led by the People's Alliance for Democracy (PAD), sometimes known as the Yellow Shirts. The crisis began in mid-2008, when the Cambodian government proposed to the World Heritage Committee (WHC) of the United Nation Economic Social and Cultural Organisation (UNESCO) to inscribe the ancient Brahmanic Temple of Preah Vihear on the World Heritage list, and the Thai government of Samak Sundaravej lent its support to the proposal. Several border clashes took place between Thai and Cambodian troops.

The sovereignty over the temple had first became a focal point of conflict between Thailand and Cambodia in 1959 when the Cambodian government

1

under the leadership of Prince Norodom Sihanouk demanded the Thai government withdraw its troops from the temple area. When Thailand failed to comply, Sihanouk decided to take the issue to the International Court of Justice (ICJ), which awarded the temple and the territory where it is situated to Cambodia in 1962. The verdict came as a shock to the Thai people, but the government had no choice but to abide with the Court's order. The government erected a temporary wire fence on the western and southern sides of the temple to indicate a demarcation line. The temple issue faded into the background through the period of the Vietnam War and Cambodia's subsequent civil war.

Generations of Thai people born after the 1962 case over the temple, including myself, grew up without witnessing any conflict over the temple until 2008. Most did not know about the ICJ case because it was not covered in any school textbook. I learned about the case only when I became an undergraduate student and saw copies of the court verdict lying in dust in the Thammasat University library. Very few people cared to pick it up. But 46 years after the verdict, the issue of sovereignty over the temple and its surrounding area was again allowed to damage Thai-Cambodian relations. PAD saw an opportunity to exploit the temple issue for domestic political purposes, namely to bring down a government which was perceived as a proxy of PAD's archenemy, the former prime minister Thaksin Shinawatra.

The opportunity for PAD arose when the government of Cambodia was preparing to nominate the temple for inclusion on the World Heritage List in 2008. The Thai government headed by Samak Sundaravej supported the nomination in the form of a Joint Communiqué, co-signed by the Thai foreign minister Noppadon Pattama and Cambodia's deputy prime minister Sok Anh on 18 June 2008. The WHC unanimously accepted the temple as a World Heritage site on 8 July. PAD accused Samak and Noppadon of "selling the motherland" in exchange for some business deal for Thaksin in Cambodia. The campaign led to border skirmishes and downgrading of diplomatic relations between the two countries. Noppadon was forced to resign when the Constitution Court ruled that the Joint Communiqué violated the constitution and could possibly cause Thailand to lose territory.

The Court also ordered the government to invalidate the Joint Communiqué.[1] PAD claimed a first victory in its temple campaign.

In September 2009, the PAD tried to occupy the temple grounds and drive out Cambodians occupying the area but they were blocked by Thai villagers living in the vicinity who resented that their livelihood was badly affected by closure of the temple to tourists.

In December 2009, the pro-Thaksin government fell after PAD had provoked a crisis by occupying Bangkok's international airports. A new government was formed headed by the Democrat Party which had earlier aligned itself with PAD's campaign over the temple and the World Heritage listing. In August 2010, the Democrat prime minister Abhisit Vejjajiva appeared at a PAD rally on the temple issue and sat with PAD representatives in a national televised debate.[2] Before long, PAD turned against the Abhisit government for failing to reverse the World Heritage listing, and its renewed campaign provoked another series of armed clashes between Thai and Cambodian troops in February and April 2011.

PAD was successful in exploiting nationalism, and particularly a nationalistic history of territories lost to western colonial powers in the past, to achieve its domestic political agenda without any regard for the detrimental effect on Thailand's relationship with Cambodia. This revival of nationalism and PAD's constant misinformation of the Thai public created huge obstacles in the way of a peaceful settlement with Cambodia.

What I found rather puzzling when I started to do a research on the temple saga was that the proposal to nominate the temple for World Heritage listing began in a spirit of cooperation between the Thai and Cambodian governments as a means to generate economic opportunities for both sides and to begin a process of resolving territorial disputes around the temple area. Although state agencies are often perceived as extremely conservative and rather inflexible in handling the highly sensitive issue of territorial dispute, the agencies of both countries involved in this case had reached an agreement, resulting in the Joint Communiqué in support of the nomination. This cooperation was destroyed by PAD's campaign.

PAD's allegations that the Samak government's support for the nomination was in some way linked with Thaksin's business interests in Cambodia has largely dominated the Thai public's view of the issue. But the allegations were vague and unsubstantiated, as I will elaborate in Chapter IV. This does not imply that Thaksin had no conflict of interests when he was prime minister. But while some of his domestic policies may have favoured his business empire, that does not prove that his business interests were behind the Thai-Cambodian cooperation over the temple.

More importantly, concentrating on the Thaksin issue overlooks the fact that bilateral cooperation on the temple listing had involved various Thai state agencies including the Ministry of Foreign Affairs, army, National Security Council, and Royal Survey Department, and had continued during three governments — those of Thaksin, General Surayud Julanond who was installed after an anti-Thaksin coup, and Samak Sundaravej (see Chapter III). PAD routinely accused anyone who opposed them of being paid by Thaksin, but it is implausible to believe that officials of those state agencies as well as the anti-Thaksin government of Surayud sacrificed their integrity to aid Thaksin's business in Cambodia. This study examines the role and rationale of various state agencies in the Thai-Cambodian cooperation over the temple listing.

The PAD campaign on the temple issue gained widespread support from various groups and individuals including academics, media, independent organizations, and politicians. Without this support, the PAD campaign would not have had such a significant impact. This study examines the roles of these various supporters.

The participants from civil society in the PAD campaign often claimed to fight on behalf of democracy and good governance, and yet their actions led to conflict with a neighbouring country. Scholars have often described civil society as a crucial factor contributing to democratization in ASEAN countries, especially Thailand, the Philippines, and Indonesia. Civil society organizations, especially NGOs, have been perceived as a force pressuring foreign policy-makers on issues of democracy, human rights, and human security. The growing activity of civil society organizations is often read as evidence of democratic progress which has tended to move slowly in many ASEAN states.[3] ASEAN itself has talked of moving from a state-centred organization to become a people-centred organization. One of the objectives of the new ASEAN Charter is to build a community binding the people of ten nations closer together based on common economic interest, security, and socio-cultural identity. However, the involvement of the Yellow Shirt movement in foreign policy proved detrimental to Thai-Cambodian relations both at the state-to-state and people-to-people levels. This is not to say that ASEAN should remain state-centric and shut itself off from civil society groups, many of which have been working to protect the rights of underprivileged people. But the PAD case shows that civil society does not always promote democratic principles, and does not always lead towards a people-centred approach. PAD called for the military to take a stronger role in solving the dispute, and did not hesitate to urge the army to use force against a smaller neighbour. PAD's propaganda cultivated hatred towards Cambodia, and damaged the efforts to build a community of Southeast Asian countries.

From 2005, the Yellow Shirt movement emerged as the most powerful Bangkok-based social movement. Its leaders called on the military and palace to intervene in politics, laying the groundwork for a military coup on 19 September 2006. While claiming to be the sole defenders of the national trinity of nation, Buddhism, and king, PAD occupied Government House, closed down Bangkok's international airports, and helped to engineer the overthrow of three governments. While claiming to restore Thai politics to a full democracy, PAD supported media censorship, accused its opponents of lèse majesté, and repeatedly resorted to tactics of character assassination to silence critics. PAD leaders urged the Abhisit government to use force against the Red Shirts movement, and supported the military's use of the Internal Security Act to suppress dissident voices and activities.

The questions thus arise: is a vibrant civil society always good for democracy and democratization, as conventional wisdom suggests; are the actions and ideology of Thai civil society groups civil or uncivil?

While civil society action damaged Thailand's relations with Cambodia, the Thai Foreign Ministry and military tried to prevent the situation spinning out of control, especially on the border. Army chiefs spoke carefully to avoid adding fuel to the fire. Foreign Ministry officials never showed any support for the PAD demands on the temple issue. In fact, the ministry officials had been deeply involved in the proposal for joint listing of the temple as a World Heritage site and disagreed with PAD's misinformation of the public. It is thus necessary to investigate the perception of the Thai Foreign Ministry officials and military on the Preah Vihear conflict and on the Thai-Cambodian relations in general; how did they balance their roles as defenders of the territory and promoters of economic cooperation; and how did they perceive the PAD campaign on the Preah Vihear issue.

Concepts of Complex Interdependence and (Un)civil Society

Thailand's post-Cold War relationship with other Southeast Asian countries, especially its neighbours, illustrates the operation of the "complex interdependence" concept.[4] According to Keohane and Nye, interdependence in world politics means a situation characterized by effects that are reciprocal, though not necessarily equal, among countries or among actors in different countries. These effects restrict autonomy and thus make the nature of the relationship interdependent. Though the conflict over the temple of Preah Vihear and its adjacent area resulted in several border clashes, the use of force by both Thailand and Cambodia was clearly restrained and stopped far short of a full-scale war. At the same time, the governments of both countries tried not to let the conflict affect other aspects of relations, especially trade and investment. Since the end of the Cold War, the links binding Thailand with its neighbouring countries have multiplied. The issues relevant to foreign policy have become more numerous and more diverse. Trade and investment, energy, environment, resources, cross-border migration, disease, trafficking, and other matters are crucial issues in foreign relations. Military security may remain important but no longer overshadows other issues all the time. In times of peace, other issues can rank higher than military security. Expanding economic cooperation in order to generate prosperity has become arguably the single most important factor in Thailand's foreign policy. The greater diversity of issues also means there are more actors, both state and non-state, involved in foreign affairs. Policy-makers thus have to become more sensitive to domestic demands. Foreign economic policies are more closely related with domestic economic activity than in the past. Foreign policy decision-making thus has to take into account several transitional issues and be aware that decisions may have spill-over effects in other areas.

Another useful conceptual framework is that of civil/uncivil society. Here I will not attempt to summarize the various theories of civil society, but only introduce a major debate on civil/uncivil society and democratization.

Since the late 1980s the fall of communist regimes in Eastern Europe as well as the decline of authoritarian regimes in South America and Asia have led to a new attention to the concept of civil society. Many political scientists have attributed democratic progress to the active role of civil society and its actors. Many scholarly works have described the constructive role played by civil society in the process of democratization in newly emerging democratic societies around the world. The conventional wisdom is that "active civil society is good for democracy". Alexis de Tocqueville was one of the first political theorists to argue that free associations that mediated between state and citizen made a significant contribution to a healthy democracy.[5] Larry Diamond suggests that civil society can play a significant role both in checking and balancing the exercise of state power as well as in founding and consolidating democratic regimes in formerly authoritarian states.[6] According to Robert D. Putnam, the decline of social capital as a result of the collapse of associational civil life in the United States since the 1960s poses a threat to the stability of America's multi-ethnic society and democracy.[7] Cohen and Arato see vibrant civil society as a supplement to political institutions of representative democracy.[8]

However, the optimistic assumption that strong civil society promotes democracy has increasingly been challenged both theoretically and empirically. Michael Foley and Bob Edwards question, "if civil society is a beachhead secure enough to be of use in thwarting tyrannical regimes, what prevents it from being used to undermine democratic governments?" They caution that strong civil associations could try to control the state, threaten governing institutions' ability to meet the demands of the dispossessed, and polarize society. They argue that to understand the role of civil society in the modern world, we must discern "how and under what circumstances a society's organised components contribute to political strength or political failure".[9]

Case studies of various civil society movements in post-communist Eastern Europe interestingly reveal civil society's use of violence, nationalism, and confrontational tactics with negative consequences for political society.[10] Recently in Asia, scholars have begun to pay attention to the uncivil characteristic of civil society. Verena Beittinger-Lee portrays the negative impact of various civil society organizations on the democratic process in post-Suharto Indonesia. She studies vigilantes, militias, paramilitaries, youth groups, civil security task forces, militant Islamic and other religious groups, ethno-nationalist groups, terrorist organizations, and groups involved in organized crimes.[11] In the Philippines, Mark R. Thomson points out that mass-based urban campaigns against the authoritarian and corrupt governments of Joseph Estrada and Gloria Macapagal Arroyo degenerated into assaults on democratic rule.[12]

In Thailand, the vigorous civil society movements since the 1980s have often been praised for their role in checking and balancing the state's power, exposing political corruption, and promoting participation in politics and policy making in numerous areas including land rights, poverty reduction, state-sponsored mega-projects, human rights protection, and environmental issues.[13] Anek Laothamatas argues that strengthening civil society is more crucial for democratization than economic development.[14] Dosch suggests that the vigorous activities of pro-democracy NGOs have helped to steer Thailand's state-centric foreign policy toward democratic values and human rights principles.[15] Yet the protracted political crisis since the September 2006 coup prompts a more critical reassessment of Thai civil society. The Yellow Shirts supported a military coup to topple the elected government of Thaksin Shinawatra. The movement's demands, strategies, and tactics can hardly be called peaceful and democratic. Their political ideology was biased in favour of the royalist and bureaucratic establishment, and contemptuous of the political rights of the majority poor.[16] In his excellent demystification of the role of the Thai middle class in democratization since 1992, Tamada Yoshifumi argues that the Thaksin government was toppled because "the middle class has lost their authority as the pro-democracy force and discursive power it has enjoyed since 1992".[17] Non-state actors can be both civil and uncivil. Civil society bodies do not necessarily have an inbuilt democratic character. Their behaviour and ideology can be uncivil and detrimental to democracy.

Scholars have begun to define "uncivil society" as something separate from "civil society". Groups involved in violence and aggression such as nationalism, racism, illicit drugs, and human trafficking are termed uncivil society. But Kopecký and Mudde caution that the exclusion of certain organisations from the definition of civil society is theoretically untenable because all social movements and organisations, even the Ku Klux Klan, claim that their actions are right and legitimate.[18] Sometimes the criteria for separating civil and uncivil societies are rather subjective. A particular group may appear civil when it opposes a communist regime but later be condemned as uncivil when it threatens a newly established democratic regime, even though its confrontational tactics may have been the same all along. Uncivil society is best viewed as a sub-set of civil society.[19]

Another complication in the definition of civil society arises because of its relationship with political and economic society. Those who portray civil society as a vital force for democratization see it by definition as a sphere independent from the state, autonomous from partisan and electoral politics, with the ability to act as a counterweight against authoritarianism and state power.[20] But in reality civil society must have some form of relationship with the state because many civil society organisations seek to influence the state's actions. The relationship exists in various forms, such as engaging in policy formulation, lobbying, and implementation. Many NGOs in both developed and developing countries receive financial funding from governments. In the same way, civil society cannot be isolated from the market or economic production because some organisations, such as trade unions, are involved in economic projects such as collective bargaining and wage negotiation.[21]

In summary, as Kopecký and Mudde argue, civil society "is a heterogeneous, highly fluid sphere of associations and organisations", including an uncivil element. Civil society cannot be strictly divided from state, electoral politics, political party, market, and economic production. Any civil society organization has to be analysed within its political context, taking into account its objectives, mobilization strategies, its interactions with the state and other political forces, and its impact on the democratic process.[22] This study adopts this approach to analyse the PAD movement in the conflict with Cambodia over the Preah Vihear temple.

Notes

1. "Samak jibes at temple injunction", *Bangkok Post*, 7 August 2010.
2. "Govt and PAD arm reach temple accord", *Bangkok Post*, 9 August 2010.
3. Jörn Dosch, *Changing Dynamics of Southeast Asian Politics* (Boulder: Lynne Rienner, 2007), p. 63; Anek Laothammatas, ed., *Democratisation in Southeast and East Asia* (Singapore: Institute of Southeast Asian Studies, 1997).
4. Robert O. Keohane and Joseph S. Nye, *Power and Interdependence*, Third edition. (London: Longman, 2001).
5. Henk E. S. Woldring, "State and Civil Society in the Political Philosophy of Alexis de Tocqueville", *Voluntas 9*, no. 4 (1998), pp. 363–73.
6. Larry J. Diamond, "Toward Democratic Consolidation", *Journal of Democracy 5*, no. 3 (July 1994), p. 8.
7. Robert D. Putnam, "Bowling Alone: America's Declining Social Capital", *Journal of Democracy 6* (January 1995), pp. 65–78.
8. Jean L. Cohen and Andrew Arato, *Civil Society and Political Theory* (Cambridge: MIT Press, 1992).
9. Michael Foley and Bob Edwards, "The Paradox of Civil Society", *Journal of Democracy 7*, no. 3 (1996), p. 46.
10. Petr Kopecky and Cas Mudde, eds., *Uncivil Society? Contentious Politics in Post-communist Europe* (London and New York: Routledge, 2003).
11. Verena Beittinger-Lee, *(Un)Civil Society and Political Change in Indonesia* (London and New York: Routledge, 2010).
12. Mark R. Thompson, "People Power Sours: Uncivil Society in Thailand and the Philippines", *Current History* (November 2008), pp. 381–87.
13. Anek Laothamatas, *Democratisation in Southeast and East Asia*; Missingham, B., *The Assembly of the Poor in Thailand* (Chiangmai: Silkworm Books, 2003).
14. Anek Laothamatas, *Democratisation in Southeast and East Asia*, p. 17.
15. Dosch, *Changing Dynamics of Southeast Asian Politics*, p. 63.
16. See Thongchai Winichakul, "Toppling Democracy", *Journal of Contemporary Asia 38*, no. 1 (February 2008), pp. 11–37; Kengkij Kitirianglarp and Kevin Hewison, "Social Movements and Political Opposition in Contemporary Thailand", *The Pacific Review* 22, no. 4 (2008), pp. 451–77; Mark R. Thompson, "People Power Sours: Uncivil Society in Thailand and the Philippines", *Current History*, (November 2008), pp. 381–87; Pavin Chachavalpongpun, "Embedding Embittered History: Unending Conflicts in Thai-Cambodian Relations", *Asian Affairs* XLII, no. 1 (March 2012), pp. 81–102.

17. Tamada Yoshifumi, *Myths and Realities: The Democratisation of Thai Politics* (Kyoto: Kyoto University Press, 2008).
18. Petr Kopecký, "Civil Society, Uncivil Society and Contentious Politics in Post-communist Europe", pp. 11–13; Cas Mudde, "Civil Society in Post-communist Europe: Lessons from the Dark Side", pp. 160–61, in *Uncivil Society? Contentious Politics in Post-communist Europe*, edited by Petr Kopecký and Cas Mudde (London and New York: Routledge, 2003).
19. Mudde, "Civil Society in Post-communist Europe", p. 169.
20. Foley and Edwards, "The Paradox of Civil Society", p. 39.
21. Kopecký, "Civil Society, Uncivil Society", pp. 8–9; Mudde, "Civil Society in Post-communist Europe", p. 158.
22. Kopecký, "Civil Society, Uncivil Society", pp. 14–15.

CHAPTER II

The Post-Cold War Regional Integration

After the UNESCO's World Heritage Committee had granted world heritage status to the Preah Vihear temple on 7 July 2008, the relationship between Thailand and Cambodia started to head downhill. A number of reactions are worth noting here. Firstly, on 28 July, while officials from both sides were holding an urgent meeting in Siem Reap on defusing border tension, PAD organized a rally in Bangkok at which Sondhi Limthongkul addressed the temple issue. He proposed numerous measures of retaliation against Cambodia and its leaders who were condemned for being arrogant toward Thailand. These proposals were not intended for the Samak Sundaravej government, which PAD was trying to topple, but for a new government, which PAD hoped would soon replace the Samak one. Some of the interesting issues in Sondhi's proposal were:[1]

- The Thai government should set up a special taskforce to lobby the members of the UN Security Council and ask them to choose between Thailand and Cambodia.
- The Thai government should tell Thai business people to withdraw from Cambodia because Thailand did not promote trade and investment in Cambodia and the Thai government would not be able to assist them if conflict broke out.
- The Thai government should inform Thai business people in the border areas that Thailand would have to close the border if conflict broke out.
- The Thai government should inform the Cambodian government that

the disputed area around the Preah Vihear temple belonged solely to Thailand which would defend her sovereignty with all means, including war. Sondhi added that Cambodia would not dare to fight with Thailand because her economy still depended on Thailand, but if Cambodia remained stubborn, Thailand should shut down all the 40 border checkpoints along the Thai-Cambodian border and suspend all flights from Thailand to Cambodia which would impact Cambodia greatly since 70 per cent of the flights had to transit in Thailand.

Secondly, in early November 2009, when Cambodian leader Hun Sen had invited Thaksin to become his economic advisor and had refused to extradite Thaksin at the request of the Abhisit government, the relationship between the two countries reached rock bottom. The Abhisit government recalled the Thai ambassador and Cambodia reciprocated. The Thai government took a swift decision to cancel the 2001 Memorandum of Understanding on the delimitation and joint development of disputed maritime territory, and threatened to suspend financial assistance of US$41.2 million to Cambodia for a road development project to connect the border town of Chong Chom in Thailand's Surin Province to Cambodia's main highway linking Siem Reap to Phnom Penh and Ho Chi Minh City. The measure was intended as a punishment for Cambodian — something urged by PAD.[2] Moreover, the deputy prime minister, Suthep Thueksuban threatened to close the Thai-Cambodian border.[3] While this retaliation appeared to please the Thai public, and increased the prime minister's popularity rating,[4] it infuriated the Cambodian leader.

Hun Sen did not wait for the Thais to implement the loan suspension. Instead, he announced that Cambodia no longer wanted the loan because his government could afford to build the road itself. He ordered all Cambodian agencies to suspend assistance from Thailand so that Thailand would not be able to demand gratitude from Cambodia. According to Hun Sen, "it was painful for me and Cambodia to have heard the Thai government's threat to suspend the assistance and loan to Cambodia. Cambodia wants to announce that she will not receive any assistance from the Abhisit government anymore." He even challenged the Thai government to shut down the border since he believed Thailand would feel the pain no less than Cambodia.[5] No order for border closure ever came from the Abhisit government.

The actions by both the PAD leader and the Abhisit government are noteworthy because they not only reflected a nationalistic and superior attitude toward Cambodia, but also showed lack of understanding on the part of the Thai public in general as well as some political leaders of the complexity of the economic relationships that Thailand had developed with neighbouring countries since the end of the Cold War. They still believed that Cambodia was a much poorer and weaker neighbour, economically and militarily; that her economy remained largely dependent on Thailand's cooperation and assistance; that the economic sanction would be an effective punishment for Cambodia; and that the impact on Thailand would be limited to a small number of Thai traders and investors in the border area, who should be ready to sacrifice their interests for the sake of the nation. Such attitudes were a remnant of the Cold War period, when ideological conflict made the two countries enemies. After the communists took over Cambodia and Laos in 1975, Thailand had closed down all its eastern borders and prohibited all economic activities with the two communist neighbours with the intention of weakening the communist regimes politically and economically.

But several questions need to be asked. Has the post-Cold War relationship between Thailand and Cambodia remained unchanged? Does Thailand still have economic and political advantages over Cambodia that allow her to threaten Cambodia easily? Would Cambodia suffer more than Thailand from an economic blockade? This chapter will illustrate how the expansion of economic linkages between Thailand and its neighbours since the end of the Cold War has transformed the fundamental relationship from antagonism to interdependence. Thai economic policy-makers were well aware of such changing realities and understood the significance of Cambodia for Thailand's expansive economic empire.

The chapter surveys the development of economic linkages between Thailand and Cambodia in the post-Cold War era as background to the emergence of conflict over the Preah Vihear temple in mid-2008.

The Tide that Turns: The Era of Economic Cooperation

As soon as the Khmer Rouge took power in Cambodia in April 1975, the Thai Interior Ministry issued an order to close all passes along the Thai-Cambodian border. In effect, the closure outlawed all movements of people and goods across the border. In January 1979, the Vietnamese invasion of Cambodia prompted an influx of refugees into camps situated in Thai territory along the Thai-Cambodian border. Between 1981 and 1985, the government of General Prem Tinsulanonda (March 1980–August 1988) passed a decree and several orders banning trade of "strategic" merchandise with Cambodia. The aim was to weaken the Vietnamese-supported regime in Phnom Penh. The list of restricted products covered a wide range from everyday goods such as monosodium glutamate to weapons.[6]

The collapse of the communist bloc from 1979 onwards affected the Thai elites' perception of the Cambodian conflict. By the end of the 1980s the Thai Foreign Ministry's hard-line policy toward Vietnam and Phnom Penh came under challenge for being ineffective at resolving the prolonged conflict in Cambodia and for being no longer suitable for the fast growing economy of Thailand. The elected government led by General Chatichai Choonhavan (August 1988–February 1991) attempted to break the ministry's monopoly on decision-making over foreign policy, and to introduce trade as a diplomatic tactic to improve trust and good relations between Thailand and the three Indochinese countries. This approach eventually added a new aspect to relations between Thailand and Cambodia. As this period was a turning point in Thai-Cambodian relations, paving the way for the future, the changes introduced by the Chatichai administration deserve close attention.

Immediately after Chatichai assumed office, he announced a new initiative to turn Indochina from a battlefield into a market place: "In the future, the neighbouring countries such as Laos and Vietnam must be market places, not battlefields anymore. The same goes for the Cambodian problem as well. We want to see peace in Cambodia in order to develop the border trade."[7] Chatichai and his advisers explained that Thailand's booming economy required both new markets as well as new sources of raw materials for fast growing export-oriented industries. Besides, economic cooperation with other Southeast Asian states, as well as peace in the region, were essential for Thailand to deal with the emergence and growing protectionism of regional trading blocs among developed countries, such as the single market policy of the European Union and the North America Free Trade Agreement (NAFTA). Because Thailand's security, political, and economic interests had been threatened by the Cambodian problem, the government needed to seek a comprehensive settlement to the protracted conflict or at least restrict its importance to the local level. The Chatichai administration argued that foreign policy should therefore cultivate a positive attitude and mutual trust with all Indochinese countries by way of talks at the leadership level. Economic relations would generate mutual benefit and common prosperity, leading towards peaceful co-existence in the region, as well as reinforcing trends toward reform in Indochina.[8]

Initially, Chatichai's proposals for promoting commercial relations with neighbouring countries and a rapprochement towards the Hun Sen government were strongly opposed by the Foreign Ministry headed by ACM Siddhi Savetsila who had been an architect of Thai foreign policy on the Cambodian conflict since the Prem Tinsulanonda administration. However, Chatichai's move was very attractive to the Thai business sector and press who were eager to see Thailand became an economic power in the region, a gateway to Indochina, and a financial centre. Improved relations between Thailand and Vietnam paved the way for Vietnam to withdraw troops from Cambodia in September 1989 and for Hun Sen to accept a ceasefire with three Cambodian factions, as proposed by Thailand. Chatichai's diplomacy was thus an important basis for the Cambodian peace process, which eventually led to the UN-sponsored elections in 1993. Thailand's political and economic relationship with Phnom Penh developed rapidly, resulting in the restoration of a formal diplomatic relationship during the Anand Panyarachun government in 1991.[9]

The Thai Foreign Ministry, which had earlier objected to General Chatichai Choonhavan's rapprochement with the Cambodian government, became actively involved in promoting political, economic, and cultural ties with Cambodia. Subsequent Thai governments have maintained Chatichai's diplomatic and economic policy towards Cambodia as well as Laos and

Vietnam. In fact, the policy was developed into a grand strategy for Thailand to become a regional economic centre.

Thailand's Grand Strategy: Expanding Investment Empire

The spurt of economic growth which began in the late 1980s made many Thais believe that the goal of becoming an economic superpower in the region was within reach. The Thai governments' strategy for developing economic relations with countries in the region is evident in two reports: *Strategic Plan to Facilitating the Economic Cooperation Development Project in the Six-country Mekong River Basin Sub-region (Thailand, Vietnam, Laos, Cambodia, Myanmar and Yunnan Province)*, produced by the National Economic and Social Development Board Office (NESDB) in 1995;[10] and *White Paper Report: Enhancing Thailand Competitiveness in the International Arena* by the Subcommittee for Enhancing Thailand's Competitiveness (SECT) in 1995.[11]

The two reports offer the same basic vision. While the private sector is to be the key player, the government's role is to facilitate transnational agreements over such issues as minimizing trade obstacles. In order to support Thai investment in the Mekong sub-region, the Thai government should have concrete plans to develop infrastructure, establish information technology services, improve diplomatic ties with neighbouring countries, and educate Thai firms about business procedure in other countries. This strategy was supported by the Asian Development Bank, the architect of and chief financial supporter for economic integration in the Greater Mekong Sub-region.[12] The reports also outline strategic plans for Thailand to become a regional hub for transportation and telecommunication, finance and banking, tourism, and human resources development, as detailed below.[13]

A regional centre for transportation and telecommunication

According to these reports, Thailand had several advantages to become a regional centre for transportation. The Thai economy was one of the fastest growing in the world, and the political, financial and economic environment appeared stable. Geographically, Thailand was a natural gateway to the emerging markets of the Indochinese countries and Myanmar, as well as having good connections to other regions. The reports therefore argued that the Thai government should intensify efforts for Thailand to become a regional hub for land, maritime, and air transport and telecommunications. While the Thai economy in general would benefit from these projects, the impact would be greatest in the north and northeast regions, which include some of the poorest and least accessible areas. Improving roads into the Thai border provinces and across to neighbouring countries would stimulate cross-border trade, investment, and tourism between Thailand and countries in the greater Mekong region.[14]

A regional centre for financial business

The two reports also stressed that developing Thailand into a regional financial hub would facilitate financial flows to Thailand and countries in the region. Thailand's financial system should be prepared to manage the increasing business activities in the region in the coming years. Thai banks should open new branches in the region and promote facilities for international finance. Laws and regulations should be modified to facilitate regional trade and investment.[15]

A regional centre for tourism

Tourism has been a significant source of foreign revenue for Thailand for decades. In 1993, Thailand ranked twelfth highest in the world for tourism revenue. The number of visitors to Thailand increased every year — 8.65 million in 1999, 9.57 million in 2000, and 10.13 million in 2001.[16] The two reports argued that Thailand had the potential to become a centre for regional tourism because of its well-developed service facilities. New destinations in newly-opened countries with rich historical heritage and attractive natural environment would draw even more tourists from around the world to visit Thailand. The government needed to improve transportation links with neighbouring countries, especially roads and aviation, and establish agreements on tourism cooperation as well as immigration laws.[17]

A regional centre for human resources development

The two reports also argued that Thailand enjoyed an advantage over its neighbours in human resources at both labour and management levels.

Thailand had an opportunity to project herself as a centre for human resources development in neighbouring countries, taking advantage of programmes under economic cooperation schemes among countries in the Mekong sub-region basin, and thereby preparing human resources for the relocation of production bases from Thailand to its lower-wage neighbours.[18] Thailand had already provided human resources training to Cambodia, Laos, Myanmar, and Vietnam through various technical assistance projects funded by both the Thai government and international donors.

These strategies to develop Thailand as a regional centre for different functions were intended to be multi-purpose and complementary. For example, road projects would facilitate trade, investment, and tourism. The next sections examines how these strategies were pursued to develop economic cooperation between Thailand and Cambodia

Thailand's Economic Cooperation with Cambodia

Thai governments have placed great emphasis on promoting cross-border trade, especially since the Greater Mekong Sub-region programme was launched in 1992. Border trade remained an important economic link between Thailand and its neighbours. From 1992 onwards, the value of cross-border trade between Thailand and Cambodian increased impressively, but resulted in a trade deficit for Cambodia (see Tables 1 and 2). The real value of border trade was possibly much higher since the figures do not include smuggling, which was reportedly widespread especially along the stretch of land and maritime border between the provinces of Trat and Koh Kong.[19] The significance of border trade was emphasized when Thailand and other Southeast Asian countries faced an economic crisis in 1997. While the overall volume of Thai exports declined, the volume of border trade was not affected at all (see Table 2).

Trade between the two countries expanded both in value and in the variety of goods (see Table 3). Immediately after cross-border trade restarted in the early 1990s, consumer goods constituted the major Thai export to Cambodia. After Cambodian refugees started to return home, and demand for housing increased, construction goods such as cement, steel rods, tiles, and paints were ordered by both private and government sectors to build and

TABLE 1

Overall Trade between Thailand and Cambodia

(In million baht)

Year	Value of trade	Export from Thailand	Import from Cambodia	Balance of Trade
1994	9,719.5	6,542.7	3,176.8	3,365.9
1995	12,310.5	8,323.9	3,986.6	4,337.3
1996	10,400.4	9,190.0	1,210.4	7,979.6
1997	11,825.1	9,620.0	2,205.1	7,414.9
1998	13,413.3	12,402.6	1,010.7	11,391
1999	13,939.1	13,382.2	556.9	12,825.3
2000	14,665.4	14,848.8	316.6	14,032.1
2001	21,316.4	20,771.2	545.1	20,226.1
2002	22,622.3	22,140.8	481.5	21,659.3
2003	29,186.1	28,678.5	507.6	28,170.9
2004	30,223.3	29,110.6	1,112.7	27,997.9
2005	36,867.6	38,137.7	1,270.1	36,867.6

Source: Department of Foreign Trade, Ministry of Commerce.

repair homes, schools, hospitals, housing, and shops. Demand for transport goods such as bicycles and motorcycles also increased as both government and private business became more active, and petrol figured in the list of the top ten exports from Thailand to Cambodia.[20] The increase in the value and variety of Thai exports to Cambodia meant that more companies and people in Thailand became involved in cross-border economic activities. Any disruption to this flow would have more widespread consequences for Thai companies and workers than was experienced when Thailand suspended economic links with Cambodia during the Cold War period.

Other Economic Players in Cambodia

Since the early 1990s steady growth in the Cambodian economy attracted more foreign direct investment (FDI). Thai investors were among the first.

TABLE 2
Cross-border Trade between Thailand and Cambodia
(In million baht)

Year	Value of trade	Export from Thailand	Import from Cambodia	Balance of Trade
1992	2,791.01	369.07	2,421.94	−2,052.87
1993	3,699.90	1,861.83	1,838.07	23.76
1994	3,914.45	2,195.91	1,718.54	477.37
1995	6,397.80	3,200.68	3,197.12	3.56
1996	5,840.49	4,555.87	1,284.62	3,271.25
1997	8,271.32	6,079.16	2,192.16	3,887.00
1998	10,040.84	9,018.77	1,022.07	7,996.70
1999	10,495.83	9,885.08	610.75	9,274.33
2002	18,850.00	18,383.76	466.24	17,917.52
2003	17,782.02	16,794.20	987.82	15,806.38
2004	23,529.70	22,083.17	1,446.53	20,636.64
2005	30,948.02	29,523.82	1,424.20	28,099.62
2006	36,173.37	34,813.15	1,360.22	33,452.93
2007	37,479.06	35,424.93	2,054.13	33,370.80

Source: Department of Foreign Trade, Ministry of Commerce, Thailand.

In 1992, the Cambodian government approved 79 Thai investment projects, the highest number among foreign countries at the time (see Table 4). By 2003–5, however, FDI from China topped the chart (see Table 5), and in 2007 the value of FDI from Vietnam ranked number one at US$53,544,330, much higher than US$13,800,000 from Thailand.[21]

Other ASEAN members, such as Singapore and Malaysia, have also developed significant economic stakes in Cambodia. By the first half of 2010, Singapore's bilateral trade with Cambodia reached S$1.3 billion, a 62 per cent increase over the same period of 2009. Singapore's investments in Cambodia have also been on the rise, multiplying eightfold in 2009 to reach US$278 million, and bringing Singapore's cumulative investments over

TABLE 3

Cross-border Import and Export Products between Thailand and Cambodia in 1999

(In million baht)

Ranking	Export from Thailand		Ranking	Import from Cambodia	
	Designation	Value		Designation	Value
1	Motorcycles and parts	765.58	1	Processed wood	760.89
2	Sugar	657.33	2	Salted cattle skin	160.61
3	Cement	633.33	3	Dried squid	25.18
4	Monosodium glutamate	303.65	4	Metal scraps	22.26
5	Drinks and soft drinks	289.15	5	Salted fish	17.64
6	Steel rods	256.07	6	Bamboo	8.34
7	Fuel oil	226.44	7	Rattan	7.49
8	Tiles	218.30	8	Machines and parts	3.92
9	Tires	177.99	9	Logs	2.44
10	Fertilizer	173.75	10	Fresh and frozen fish	2.24

Source: Department of Foreign Trade, Ministry of Commerce

TABLE 4

Approved Foreign Investment in Cambodia as of April 1992

Country	Number of Projects
Thailand	79
France	61
Hong Kong	59
Singapore	35
U.S.A	20
Taiwan	19
Hungary	10
Australia	6
Japan	4
Malaysia	2

Note: Excluding agreements signed with Thai provincial authorities or Cambodian resistance factions.

Source: Thailand Board of Investment, *Investment in Cambodia*, n.d.

fifteen years to US$604 million, the eighth highest among Cambodia's foreign investors.[22] Meanwhile Malaysia's investments over 1996–2010 totalled US$2.19 billion. When Prime Minister Najib Razak visited Cambodia in May 2010, he led several dozen business people to meet with counterparts in Phnom Penh where they concluded six deals worth more than a billion US dollars. One deal on information communication security alone was worth US$700 million, while other projects included expansion of a KFC fast food franchise, a chicken farm, twenty bistro shops, a joint venture in halal food, a technical and training exchange programme, and strengthening the Malaysia-Cambodia Business Council.[23]

Thailand is thus no longer a dominant foreign investor in Cambodia. The increasing number of foreign players gives the country more alternatives and some insurance in case the relationship with Thailand goes awry.

Between 1994 and 2004, the main sector for Thai investors was the food processing industry, with nine projects. But the sector which drew the highest value of FDI was tourism (including hotels and restaurants), most of which

TABLE 5

FDI in Cambodia between 2003 and 2005*

(In million U.S. dollar)

Country	2003		2004		2005	
	Registered fund	%	Registered fund	%	Registered fund	%
China	14.2	47.2	23.8	47.0	237.8	79.3
Korea	1.1	3.7	4.2	8.3	15.7	5.2
Thailand	3.1	10.3	2.0	3.9	14.8	4.9
Malaysia	3.7	12.3	7.8	15.4	10.7	3.6
Australia	0.6	2.0	N/A	N/A	7.0	2.3
Others	7.5	25.0	12.9	25.4	14.0	4.7
Total	30.2	100	50.66	100	300	100

* Joint investment with local investors and other foreign investors.

Source: Office of Foreign Trade Promotion in Phnom Penh, Ministry of Commerce, 2003, quoted from Thai Chamber of Commerce University, *Handbook for Investment in Cambodia*. Report presented to Thailand Board of Investment (Bangkok: 2006), p. 78.

was located in Siem Reap. Other interesting sectors for Thai business were textiles and garments, wood-processing, agro-industry, construction, and telecommunications (see Table 6). However, the numbers shown in Table 6 appear to capture only large-scale investment, and the true value must have been higher since many small and medium enterprises, such as restaurants and hairdressers, were not required to seek government approval and are thus not registered. In 2006 the Thai Business Council in Cambodia had 111 company members, mostly in the restaurant and trading sectors.

Thailand's Strategies in Cambodia

The Abhisit government's announcement about suspending financial aid to Cambodia in late 2009 must be seen not only in the context of the expanded economic linkages between the two countries, but also against the background of foreign policy in recent years. Since economic relations between the two countries were restored in late 1980s, Thai government

TABLE 6

Thai Investments in Cambodia Approved by Cambodia Investment Board, August 1994 and 30 September 2004

(In U.S. Dollar)

	Type	No. of projects	Registered fund	Fund from Thailand
1	Hotel	7	123,400,000	43,383,350
2	Wood Processing	3	38,000,000	33,920,000
3	Communication	2	16,000,000	14,800,000
4	Garment	7	8,050,000	7,720,000
5	Food Processing	9	7,660,000	5,765,000
6	Construction	5	7,334,000	4,538,000
7	Agro-industry	5	11,295,000	4,395,000
8	Plastic	3	4,300,000	3,260,000
9	Media	4	2,760,000	2,696,000
10	Mines	3	3,040,000	2,250,000
11	Air Traffic Control	1	2,5000,000	2,250,000
12	Assembly Plant	1	2,000,000	2,000,000
13	Chemical Products	2	1,400,000	890,000
14	Petroleum	3	1,550,000	820,000
15	Packaging	1	650,000	650,000
16	Entertainment	1	5,000,000	500,000
	Total	57	234,939,000	135,152,350

Source: Cambodia Investment Board, quoted from Thai Chamber of Commerce University, *Handbook for Investment in Cambodia*. Report presented to Thailand Board of Investment (Bangkok: 2006), p. 84.

agencies had become involved in projects to improve transportation links with a clear objective of facilitating Thailand's export to and investment in Cambodia.[24]

In theory, Thailand should have a competitive edge over trading rivals from Singapore, Malaysia, Vietnam and China because of its proximity to Cambodia, realizing that competitive advantage depended on good access from the Thai border into Cambodia.

From the early 1990s, Thai Army engineers helped repair the abandoned Aran-Poipet railway. They also built the Poipet-Sisophon road, the Ban Hat Lek-Koh Kong road with a new bridge across the Satung Krangkruen, and a new 153 km. road from Koh Kong to Sre Ambel with four river crossings. The long awaited Bangkok-Aranyaprathet-Phnom Penh-Ho Chi Minh-Vung Tau Road improvement project, funded by an Asian Development Bank loan, facilitated wider distribution of Thai exports to the Mekong sub-region. An ADB-sponsored project for a road along the coastline of Thailand-Cambodia-Vietnam was recently completed.[25]

After Thailand had recovered from the 1997 economic crisis, a strategic plan to relocate Thai manufacturing industry into neighbouring countries started to gain serious consideration from Thai state agencies. A million illegal migrants had entered Thailand from neighbouring countries, and were viewed as a serious threat to economic and social stability. The relocation of production bases was intended to reduce the flow of migrants by creating jobs in the host countries, while simultaneously allowing Thai manufacturers to access markets for labour-intensive products under the General System of Preferences (GSP) which had been closed to Thailand in 2002. The plan became part of the Ayeyawady-Chao Phraya-Mekong Economic Cooperation Strategy (ACMECS) launched by the Thaksin government.[26]

The Thai and Cambodian government began planning to develop industrial zones on the Thai-Cambodian border. In June 2000, Bangkok and Phnom Penh agreed to formulate an integrated plan for this purpose. The zones would be located in Cambodia close to the Thai border in order to take advantage of the better Thai infrastructure, especially road and rail links to the Laem Chabang port on the Eastern Seaboard. Thai manufacturers would benefit from the lower labour costs in Cambodia that were approximately half the rate of labour on the Thai side of the border. A site at Neang Kok on Cambodia's coastline in Koh Kong province, two kilometres from the Thai border, was designated for the development of an industrial zone. The site is three hours by road from Laem Chabang port. Another site being considered was at Poipet, close to Cambodia's second biggest city, Battambang.[27]

After the 1997 economic crisis, Thai governments gave assistance for improvement of several roads from the Thai border into Cambodia in order to facilitate cross-border economic activities.

1. In March 2000, the Chuan Leekpai cabinet approved a budget for improvement of the 48-kilometre Poipet-Banteay Meanchey Road, which links to the Banteay Meanchey-Siem Reap and Banteay Meanchey-Battambang-Phnom Penh roads.

2. The Cambodian government requested Thailand's assistance for developing the 50-kilometre Sre Snom-Kralanh road, which is an extension from the Chong Chom-O Smet pass on the border to Oddar Meanchey and Kralanh.[28]

3. In May 2003, the Thaksin government granted a low interest loan and funds for an economic and environmental assessment study on the construction of four bridges for development of Road Number 48 which connects Koh Kong-Sre Ambel to RN 4 to Phnom Penh.

4. In June 2003, the Thaksin cabinet approved aid to improve the 151-kilometre RN 67 between Thailand's Chong Sa-ngam and Cambodia's Anlong Veng-Siem Reap route. The aid consisted of two parts: funding for design and construction of the road and improvement of the part in poor condition; and a low-interest loan for improving the Anlong Veng-Siem Reap connection.[29]

5. In July 2009, another low interest loan of US$41.2 million was earmarked for developing RN 68 in order to boost tourism and trade between the two countries.

Though in early November 2009 Abhisit had made a swift announcement on suspending a loan for road construction in Cambodia, he later changed his mind. The suspension seems partly to have been an emotional retaliation to Hun Sen, who was perceived by the Thai media and general public as an arrogant neighbour. Abhisit obviously wanted to please the widespread anti-Cambodia sentiment among the Thai public. Later the government seems to have reconsidered in view of the significance of economic links with Cambodia for the well-being of Thai economy. Though Abhisit repeatedly played the nationalist card, he did not want to interrupt cross-border economic activities. Behind the scenes of the blazing conflict over the temple, his cabinet was engaged in promoting economic ties with Cambodia.

Soon after the two countries agreed to normalize their diplomatic ties by reinstating their ambassadors on 25 August 2010, the Abhisit cabinet unveiled several economic plans concerning Cambodia. On the same day, Thailand pledged to resume the loan for developing a road from the Thai border to Phnom Penh and Ho Chi Minh City.[30] The next day, the deputy commerce minister Alongkorn Ponlaboot led a business mission to Phnom Penh and Ho Chi Minh City to study road transport and logistics development. The mission was part of Thailand's plan to raise the value of border trade by 40 per cent within three years.[31] As Thailand's investment in Cambodia had fallen behind China and Vietnam in recent years, the Abhisit cabinet pledged to regain Thailand's leadership within five years. According to Alongkorn, the key to achieve this ambition was to capitalize on the potential of Cambodia's RN 5, which was the land gateway to Vietnam.[32] The cabinet also announced a plan to develop a special economic zone in the border province of Sa Kaeo, to be jointly developed by the Thai and Cambodian governments to promote more border trade and investment.[33] Plans for more border checkpoints were also announced.[34] Thailand's policy-makers believed that friendly relations with neighbouring countries were vital for Thailand's industrial development. The NESDB proposed moving industries into neighbouring countries because Thailand could not accommodate more heavy industries, such as upstream steel projects. The country's biggest industrial complex in Laem Chabang had become overcrowded and so severely polluted that it was facing opposition from local communities. Koh Kong Province of Cambodia was one of the prospective areas for relocation of Thai industries.[35]

Aid as a Soft Power

Apart from financial aid, Thai governments in the early 1990s also offered technical assistance to Cambodia as well as to Laos, Myanmar, and Vietnam in the form of training and scholarships in various fields such as agriculture, medicine, livestock, education, public health, management, and tourism. In 1991, on the initiative of the Foreign Affairs Ministry, the cabinet of Anand Panyarachun began to promote aid and technical assistance as an instrument of foreign policy toward neighbouring countries. From the early 1990s, aid and technical assistance were offered to Cambodia as part of the strategy to enhance Thailand's competitiveness in the global market. In other words, it was an extension of Thailand's strategy to become an economic superpower in the region. The NESDB explicitly stated that aid and technical assistance to neighbours should be understood as measures to promote Thailand's economic relations with those countries.[36]

Against the background of a booming Thai economy, the Anand administration believed Thailand was ready to move from being an aid recipient to becoming an aid donor to her poorer neighbours and thus promoting Thailand's international status. The value of aid and assistance gradually increased from this time (see Table 7). This vision was later endorsed by the Thaksin government.

However, unstable diplomatic relations between Thailand and Cambodia remained a sensitive issue and affected Thai business in Cambodia. Thai state agencies were aware that Thailand needed to win the hearts of its Indochinese neighbours, who had long histories of antagonism with Thailand.[37] In January 2003, a misquoted remark by a Thai actress provoked a riot in Phnom Penh during which the Thai embassy and Thai businesses came under attack. This incident reconfirmed the fragility of the relationship between the two countries and sent a message that a strong commitment was needed to improve ties between the two countries. Thai state agencies believed aid should be employed to build trust and goodwill among people of neighbouring countries.[38] Thailand needed to exert soft power in order to win the hearts and minds of her neighbours.

TABLE 7
Value of Technical Assistance to Thailand's Neighbours
(In million baht)

Year	Laos	Cambodia	Vietnam	Myanmar
1992	42.5	20	20	21
1993	54.5	30	17.4	41.5
1994	91.5	16	25	28.7
1995	119.1	40	50	55
1996	126.2	45	37	16.1
1997	176.6	56	48	24.8
1998	69.1	44.5	34.6	19
1999	79	15	15	4

Source: Thailand International Development Cooperation Agency, 2006.

However, the value of the financial assistance that Thailand offered to Cambodia was much smaller than that from Japan or China.[39] In addition, after the 1993 UN-sponsored general election, international financial organizations such as the World Bank, International Monetary Fund, and Asian Development Bank had started to channel funding into Cambodia. The financial and technical assistance Thailand offered to Cambodia was thus a gesture of goodwill and friendship rather than a substantial contribution to Cambodia's economic recovery (see Table 8). The Abhisit government's cancellation of aid in retaliation against Hun Sen was a bad miscalculation of the political and economic realities. This response portrayed Thailand's attitude of superiority towards smaller neighbours, and encouraged the Thai public to believe that Thailand was in a position to inflict economic punishment on a neighbour without any consequences for herself. In fact, this retaliation was not only ineffective but exacerbated the hostility between the peoples and leaders of the two countries. Above all, it ran counter to the primary strategy, pursued by successive Thai governments since the end of the Cold War, of cultivating friendship with neighbouring countries.

Summary

Following the end of the Cold War, Thai foreign policy decision-makers no longer perceived its former communist neighbours of Cambodia, Laos and Vietnam as archenemies, but as potential economic partners. In the age of globalization, policy-makers positioned Thailand as the leader and centre of economic cooperation in the region. They believed Thailand was in a better position than other countries to capitalize on these emerging markets, and they launched several schemes of economic cooperation with neighbouring countries, both bilateral and multilateral. From 1995 onwards, Thailand's exports to ASEAN markets exceeded those to Japan, the European Union, or the US.[40] (See Table 9.)

Economic linkages between Thailand and Cambodia expanded both in value and variety. Cambodia became an important market and investment area for Thailand's economic empire. Trade expanded along with Cambodia's increasing demand for consumer products. But while Thailand was the

TABLE 8

Cambodia's GDP Real Growth Rate (%)

Country	2000	2001	2002	2003	2004	2005	2006	2007	2008	2009	2010
Cambodia	4	5.3	5.2	5	5.4	13.4	7.2	10.1	5	–1.5	6

Source: Index Mundi. Retrieved from <http://www.indexmundi.com/g/g.aspx?v=66&c=cb&l=en> (accessed 6 April 2012).

TABLE 9

Thailand's Export to Several Regional Markets, 1995–2010

(Value: US$ million)

Year	ASEAN (9)	Japan	The U.S.	The EU (27)	Others
1995	12,325.26	9,524.75	10,113.15	9,295.40	15,466.74
1996	12,113.37	9,417.05	10,061.31	9,246.90	15,102.82
1997	12,734.19	8,837.41	11,341.11	9,659.11	15,757.58
1998	9,895.85	7,469.33	12,167.20	10,008.71	14,948.97
1999	10,871.61	8,261.32	12,654.27	10,110.41	16,565.83
2000	13,482.22	10,232.38	14,870.11	11,378.74	19,660.77
2001	12,599.12	9,945.38	13,199.62	10,912.61	18,526.50
2002	13,568.90	9,949.98	13,509.42	10,590.03	20,537.99
2003	16,486.03	11,356.20	13,569.16	12,217.19	26,384.42
2004	21,238.38	13,491.63	15,502.86	14,445.84	31,824.11
2005	24,390.42	15,098.85	16,996.64	15,100.07	39,360.67
2006	27,021.71	16,385.90	19,449.60	18,006.24	48,856.98
2007	32,791.08	18,119.05	19,415.61	21,688.17	61,851.05
2008	40,151.28	20,093.64	20,274.76	23,392.07	73,863.46
2009	32,498.67	15,723.68	16,661.26	18,153.63	69,398.05
2010	44,333.56	20,411.82	20,200.45	21,814.56	88,546.30

Source: Centre for Information and Communication Technology, Office of Secretary General of Ministry of Commerce <www.ops.3moc.go.th/export/market_export/report.asp> (accessed 19 October 2011).

primary supplier of consumer goods and a significant investor, this did not mean that Thailand had any control over the Cambodian economy. If trade between the two countries were disrupted, Cambodia could always turn to other countries such as Vietnam and China, which export similar products as those from Thailand.

The expansion of economic linkages between Thailand and neighbouring countries since the end of the Cold War transformed the fundamental character of the relationship from enmity to economic interdependence. Any interruption in economic ties would affect both countries. Thailand can no longer act unilaterally without being seriously affected by her own decision. Besides, the age of globalization has given Cambodia more international linkages which can serve as alternatives to Thailand. Cambodia can always turn to other potential international partners. The increase in cooperation and assistance from other countries allowed the Cambodian leader to be confident in dealing with Thailand. In reaction to Abhisit's suspension of financial aid, Hun Sen not only suspended *all* aid from Thailand but pointedly criticized the coup origins of the Abhisit government. This criticism may have outraged many Thais, but it is important for the Thai leaders and the Thai public to understand the basis of the Cambodian leader's confidence and the increasingly interdependent nature of the Thai-Cambodian relationship.

While the Thai political leaders, including the PAD leaders, may base their actions on short-term political calculation rather than an informed view of the political and economic realities, those involved in the foreign policy making process, such as the NESDB and Foreign Ministry, were well aware of these changed realities, as indicated by the trends of foreign policy in recent years, as described above. The cooperation between the Cambodian and Thai governments over the listing of the Preah Vihear temple as a World Heritage site took place within Thailand's grand strategy for cross-border cooperation with her neighbours. This issue will be discussed in the next chapter.

Notes

1. "Kankaekhai panha khaophrawihan baep sonthi limthongkun" [Solving the problem of the temple of Preah Vihear in Sondhi Limthongkul's style], *Prachatai*, 28 July 2008 <http://prachatai.com/journal/2008/07/17535> (accessed 8 October 2008).
2. "Cancel other pacts, financial aid projects to Cambodia, PAD urges", *Bangkok Post*, 8 November 2009.
3. "Hun sen krao mi rueang kap Mak doi trong" [Hun Sen toughens, having problem with Abhisit only], *Matichon*, 11 November 2009.
4. "Abhisit's govt needs to redefine the national interest", *Bangkok Post*, 19 November 2009.
5. "Khaeo ratthaban mi mue nueng kae panha khamen" [Mocking, the government has the best hand to solve problem with Cambodia], *Matichon*, 2 December 2009; "An tem tem kham samphat khong Hun Sen lae kan topto chak krasuang

kantangprathet khong thai" [Read in full, Hun Sen's interview and the response from the Thai Foreign Ministry], *Prachatai*, 11 November 2009 <http://prachatai. com/journal/2009/11/26539> (accessed 11 November 2009).

6. Watcharin Yongsiri et al., *Kankha thai-indochin* [*The Thai-Indochinese trade*] (Bangkok: Asian Studies Institute, Chulalongkorn University, 1992), pp. 95, 128–30 and Appendices 14–21.

7. *Sayam Rath*, 5 August 1988.

8. Puangthong Rungswasdisab, "Thailand's Response to the Cambodian Genocide", in *Genocide in Cambodia and Rwanda: New Perspectives*, edited by Sue Cook (New Brunswick: Transaction, 2006), pp. 73–118.

9. Ibid.

10. Office of the National Economic and Social Development Board (hereafter NESDB), *Phaen yuttasat phuea rong rap khrongkan pattana khwamruammue thang settakit nai anuphumiphak maenamkhong hok pratet (thai wiatnam lao kamphucha phama lae monthonyunnan)* [Strategic Plan to Facilitating the Economic Cooperation Development Project in the Six-country Mekong River Basin Sub-region (Thailand, Vietnam, Laos, Cambodia, Myanmar and Yunnan Province)] (Bangkok, 1995).

11. Sub-committee for Enhancing Thailand's Competitiveness (hereafter SETC), *Samutpokkhao kanphoem kitkhwamsamat naikankhaengkan kap tangprathet* [White Paper Report: Enhancing Thailand Competitiveness in the International Arena] (Bangkok, 1995).

12. See Asian Development Bank's projects in the Greater Mekong Sub-region at <www.adb.org/GMS/projects/adb-projects.asp>.

13. NESDB, *Strategic Plan*, pp. 6-21; SETC, *White Paper*, pp. 59–69.

14. NESDB, *Strategic Plan*, pp. 6-3–6-4; SETC, *White Paper*, pp. 59–62.

15. NESDB, *Strategic Plan*, pp. 6-4; SETC, *White Paper*, pp. 65–67.

16. Watcharin Yongsiri, *Kan kha chaidaen thai kap kamphucha panha thiprasop naipatchuban lae naewthang kaekhai* [Border trade between Thailand and Cambodia: problems and solutions- hereafter cited as *Border Trade*] (Bangkok: Asian Studies Institutes, Chulalongkorn University, 2004), p. 165.

17. NESDB, *Strategic Plan*, pp. 6-4 – 6-5; SETC, *White Paper*, pp. 64–69.

18. NESDB, *Strategic Plan*, pp. 6-5.

19. Watcharin Yongsiri, *Border Trade*, p. 86.

20. Watcharin Yongsiri, *Border Trade*, p. 276.

21. Thailand Board of Investment, "Trade and Investment in Cambodia", at <www. boi.go.th/thai/clma/2009_cambodia_d5_5-1html> (accessed 24 July 2009).

22. Ministry of Trade and Industry Singapore, "Mr Lim Hng Kiang at the Luncheon with Singapore Business Community in Honour of Samdech Akka Moha Sena Padei Techo Hun Sen PM of the Kingdom of Cambodia, 26 July 2010"

<http://app.mti.gov.sg/default.asp?id=148&articleID=22482> (accessed 6 April 2012).

23. "Cambodia, Malaysia pledge to further trade, investment relations", *People's Daily Online*, 12 May 2010 <http://english.people.com.cn/90001/90778/9085 8/90863/6982055.html> (accessed 16 April 2012).

24. An estimated 30 per cent of Thai exports via border trade were distributed to wholesalers and retailers in the provinces along the way to Phnom Penh, such as Battambang, Pursat, and Kampong Chhanang, and around half of the remainder was re-exported to southern Vietnam. See Watcharin Yongsiri, *Border Trade*, pp. 181–82.

25. Watcharin Yongsiri, *Border Trade*, p. 181; NESDB, *Progress and Direction for Developing Special Economic Zone and Economic Corridor to Neighbouring Countries* (Bangkok: 2001), p. 3.

26. ACMECS, "ACMECS Projects", <http://www.acmecs.org/index.php?id=124> (accessed 20 May 2006).

27. International Chamber of Commerce, the United Nations, *An Investment Guide to Cambodia: Opportunities and Conditions* (2004), p. 43.

28. Watcharin Yongsiri, *Border Trade*, p. 173.

29. Watcharin Yongsiri, *Border Trade*, p. 73; Ministry of Foreign Affairs, Thailand, "The Kingdom of Cambodia" <www.mfa.go.th/web/479.php?id=51> (accessed 10 May 2006).

30. "Road funds for Cambodia unfrozen", *Bangkok Post*, 27 August 2010.

31. "Tri-nation highway tour", *Bangkok Post*, 28 August 2010.

32. "Diplomacy set to pay dividend in Cambodia", *Bangkok Post*, 6 September 2010.

33. "Govt plans special economic zone", *Bangkok Post*, 30 August 2010.

34. "Govt pushes new border checkpoints", *Bangkok Post*, 28 September 2010.

35. "Neighbours recommended for heavy-industry projects", *Bangkok Post*, 18 August 2010.

36. NESDB, *Strategic Plan*, pp. 6-20 – 6-21; SETC, *White Paper*.

37. University of Thai Chamber of Commerce, *Study on Investment Promotion for Thai Business Sector in Laos, Cambodia and Myanmar*. Paper presented to Thailand Board of Investment (Bangkok: 2004), pp. 4–9.

38. Department of Policy and Planning, Ministry of Foreign Affairs, *Report on the Foreign Ministry Works in accordance with the Cabinet Policy October 1993–October 1993* (Bangkok: n.d.), p. 23.

39. In 2006, China granted US$600 million in financial assistance to Cambodia. In the same year, the total value of Japan's aid to Cambodia was US$106.28 million. See Chheng Vannarith, *Cambodia: Between China and Japan* Working paper no. 31 (Cambodian Institute of Cooperation and Peace, 2009) <http://www.cicp.

org.kh/download/CICP%20Working%20series/CICP%20Working%20Paper%
20No%2031_Cambodia_Between%20China%20and%20Japan%20by%20Cheang
%20Vannarith.pdf> (accessed 20 October 2011).

40. Centre for Information and Communication Technology, Office of Secretary
General of Ministry of Commerce <www.ops.3moc.go.th/export/market_
export/report.asp> (accessed 19 October 2011).

CHAPTER III

Thai-Cambodian Cooperation on the Preah Vihear Temple

The Thai-Cambodian Joint Communiqué, an agreement between Thailand and Cambodia to promote the Preah Vihear temple as a World Heritage site, was signed on 18 June 2008 by the Thai foreign minister Noppadon Pattama and his Cambodian counterpart Sok Anh. Noppadon had earlier been a lawyer for Thaksin Shinawatra. The Thai government coalition at the time was headed by the pro-Thaksin People Power Party, though Thaksin himself was in self-imposed exile. The anti-Thaksin movement later claimed that Thaksin and his proxies had "sold the motherland" in exchange for Thaksin's business advance in Cambodia. Using nationalist rhetoric, the movement claimed Thailand would gain nothing from the inclusion of the temple on the World Heritage list other than a little tourist business in the temple vicinity; meanwhile Thailand risked losing sovereignty over 4.6 square kilometres of land around the temple to Cambodia.

This allegation dominated the Thai public's perception of the conflict over the temple. But, as I have elaborated in the previous chapter, the temple was only one issue in the fast developing and multidimensional relations between Thailand and Cambodia since the early 1990s. This is not to say that Thaksin had no business interest in Cambodia, but until now no proof has been produced so the allegation remains hearsay. Some of PAD's claims were simply fiction, as I will discuss in the next chapter. Moreover, Thaksin's background as a transnational businessman and the conflict of interest evident in some of his domestic policies should not overshadow the development of Thai-Cambodian relations in the last two decades. In other words, it is imperative to consider the temple issue within the context of Thai-Cambodian socio-economic relations since the end of the Cold War. The bilateral cooperation over the temple of Preah Vihear was not the decision of one man but involved several successive governments and several state agencies in charge of economic affairs, foreign affairs, and national security. In this chapter I will analyse the rationale behind Thai state agencies' support for Cambodia's proposal to inscribe the temple on the World Heritage list within the framework of economic linkages between the two countries discussed in the previous chapter. Bilateral cooperation over the temple was a progressive step by Thai and Cambodian decision-makers in handling a territorial dispute with economic and cultural means.

First of all, it is necessary to understand the background of the dispute between Thailand and Cambodia over the Preah Vihear temple and its 4.6 square kilometre surrounding area because these issues were manipulated and misrepresented in the PAD's campaign. The following section will provide details of the International Court of Justice's verdict, its implication, the nomination of the temple for the World Heritage list, and the dispute over the surrounding area of the temple.

The 1962 Court Verdict

The temple of Preah Vihear is an Angkorean-era sanctuary and shrine, dedicated to the Hindu god Shiva. It is perched on the southern end of a 625-meter high rock promontory of the Dongrek (or Dongrak) mountain range, bordering Thailand and Cambodia. Considerable portions of the Dongrek range consist of a high cliff-like escarpment rising abruptly above the Cambodian plain. From the top of this steep escarpment, the temple looks to the south over a vast plain stretching out below on the Cambodian side. Beyond the plateau to the north, the terrain extends in a gentle slope towards Thailand. The architecture of the temple presents a north-south axial plan. The distance from the access on the north to the mountain top on the south is approximately 896 meters.[1] The complex consists of five "gopuras" (gateways) linked by a series of stairways and corridors with several ancillary buildings basins, and reservoirs, leading to the main sanctuary situated at the highest and southernmost point close to the edge of the escarpment (see Picture 1). The convenient and best-known access is from present day Thailand to the north. But there are also two roads, formerly abandoned, connecting Cambodian towns to the eastern and western sides of the temple. Recently, the Cambodian government has developed these two roads and other tourist facilities after the temple became a World Heritage site in July 2008.

Apart from the temple complex proposed by the Cambodian government to be listed as a World Heritage site, there are other archaeological sites which are related to the temple but are situated in territory claimed by Thailand. These include Sa Trao, an ancient reservoir, and a small bas-relief engraved on natural sandstone depicting a Shiva Lingam enclosed within a Yoni Base.

After the decline of the Angkorean Empire in the 15th century, the Preah Vihear temple was largely forgotten, possibly known only to the local villagers. The international community learnt about the temple when the Cold War inflamed the relationship between Thailand and Cambodia. After Cambodia gained independence in 1953, the government of Prince Norodom Sihanouk sent officials to oversee the temple and found Thai armed forces already there. Sihanouk sent a number of notes to the Thai government of Field Marshall Sarit Thanarat, demanding the withdrawal of Thai personnel from the area, but received no response from the Thai side.[2] With the Cold War in the background, the Thai government chose to side with the United States, while Sihanouk announced that Cambodia would remained neutral. Washington and Bangkok were displeased by Sihanouk's stance, and this hostility gave rise to the territorial dispute. In mid 1958, Sihanouk's government demanded the Thai government remove its forces from the temple and its vicinity. Both sides exchanged verbal assaults via the media. Tension along the border increased to the point that the Thai government placed all five provinces bordering Cambodia under emergency rule in August 1958. Sihanouk subsequently suspended diplomatic relations with Thailand. On 6 October 1959, Cambodia decided to take the sovereignty dispute over the temple and its precinct to the International Court of Justice (ICJ) at The Hague.

The ICJ recorded its judgment on 15 June 1962: "The Court, by nine votes to three, finds that the temple of Preah Vihear is situated in territory

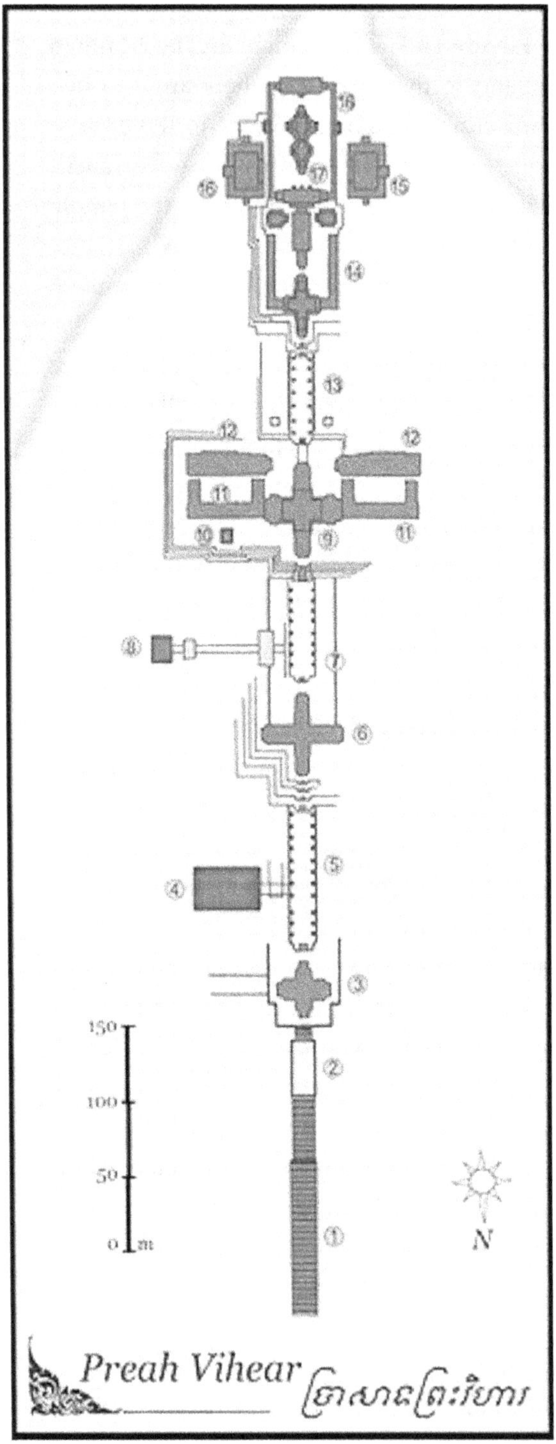

Picture 1: Main structure of the temple of Preah Vihear

Source: <http://en.wikipedia.org/wiki/File:Preahvihear.jpg>

1. Monumental stairway
2. Naga platform
3. Gopura 1st level
4. Large reservoir
5. 1st pillared causeway
6. Gopura 2nd level
7. 2nd pillared causeway
8. Lion head reservoir
9. Gopura 3rd level
10. Tower
11. U-shaped extension
12. Palace
13. Naga balustrade
14. Gopura 4th level
15. Western building
16. Eastern building
17. Galleries
18. Sanctuary

under the sovereignty of Cambodia." The Court also ordered Thailand to withdraw forces stationed at the temple and its vicinity and return to Cambodia any objects removed from the temple.[3]

The decision caused an uproar among the Thai public which had been emotionally engaged with the trial from the beginning because of a nationalist campaign. The Sarit government had asked people to contribute one baht each to a fund for the legal team. Collections totalled three million baht.[4] The court defeat brought back a bitter memory of the loss of Thai territories in the nineteenth and early twentieth centuries to the British and French colonial powers which took away Thailand's several tributary states, including the Lao kingdoms, Cambodia, the Malay sultanates, and part of present-day Burma. Otherwise, present-day Thailand would have been much larger and stronger. This chapter of history has been an essential part of Thai historical textbooks studied by generations of Thais.[5]

Demonstrations against the ICJ verdict were held throughout the country. Students from five leading state universities led the protests in Bangkok. Even though public demonstration was illegal in Thailand at that time, the government openly approved of these instances. After half a month of public protest, however, the Sarit government had no choice but to comply with the Court order. A cabinet resolution dated 11 July 1962 ordered erection of a barbed wire fence around the area to be returned to Cambodia. On the northern side, the fence ran from the cliff edge due east passing twenty metres to the north of the Naga staircase providing entrance to the temple complex. On the western side, the fence ran due south passing one hundred metres away from the main sanctuary to the cliff edge. The area enclosed by this fence and the cliff top is only 1.4 square kilometre (see Picture 2). The fence has become a de facto demarcation line upheld by Thai governments since that time.[6]

Map, Treaties, and Area of Overlapping Claims

A disputed area on the northern and western sides of the temple has become the most critical issue in the current conflict between Thailand and Cambodia (see Picture 2). The area is the difference between two conflicting claims based on two different pieces of evidence: the treaties of 1904 and 1907 on the one hand, and the map referred to by the Court as the Annex I Map on

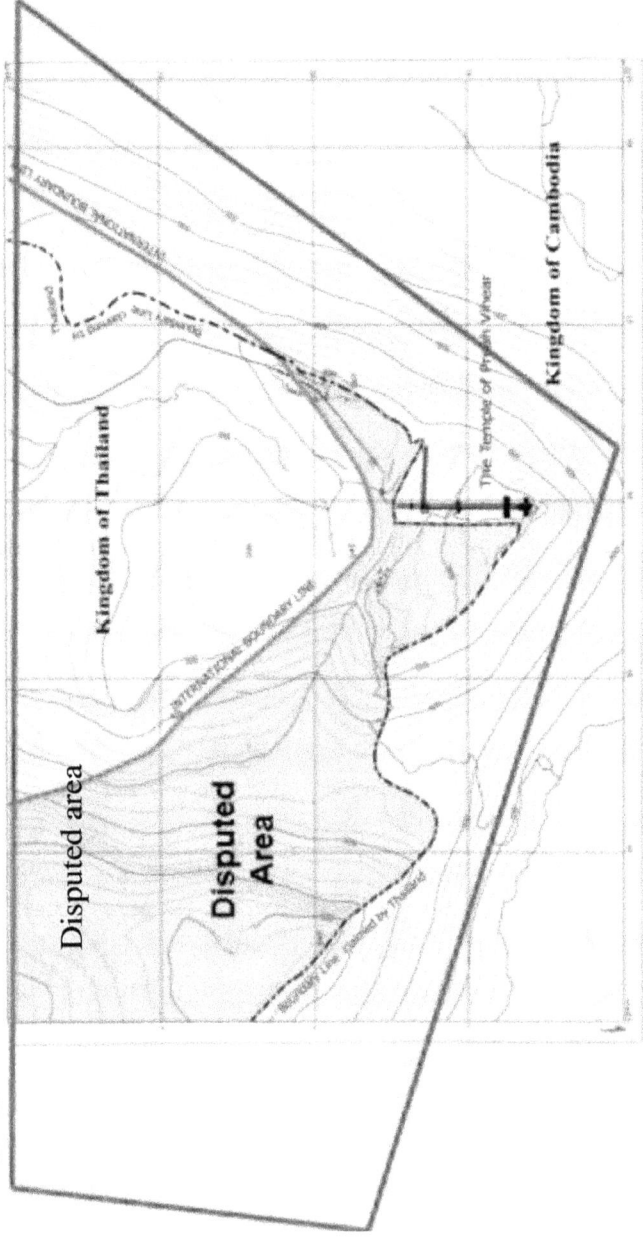

Picture 2: Disputed area adjacent to the temple of Preah Vihear.

Note: Yellow area is the disputed area. The area within the red line is a demilitarized zone created by the ICJ's provisional measure.

Source: Asian Correspondent.com <http://asiancorrespondent.com/60292/icj-decision-creates-temporary-demilitarized-zone-around-preah-vihear-temple/>

the other. Thailand claims that the boundary is defined by clauses in the treaties, while Cambodia insists on the demarcation line shown on the map. In order to understand the complexity of this point, we must examine the treaties, the map, and the ICJ verdict.

The Franco-Siamese Treaties of 13 February 1904 and of 23 March 1907 stipulated that the boundary between Siam and Thailand along the Dongrek mountain range, where the temple is situated, should follow the line of the watershed, and that a commission composed of officials appointed by the two contracting countries should map the line. However, Siam did not send a representative to the commission but allowed the French team to carry out the mapping alone. The delimitation work, completed in late 1907, yielded eleven maps covering eleven parts of the entire land frontier between Siam and French Indochina, from Laos to Cambodia. One of those eleven maps covers the Dongrek portion (and is generally known as the "Annex 1 Map"). If the delimitation work had strictly followed the watershed, as stipulated in the treaties, the temple of Preah Vihear would have fallen under Thailand's sovereignty. However, the French mapping team, possibly intentionally, located the entire promontory, including the temple, within Cambodian territory. The subsequent conflict is a legacy of this mapping.

In its petition to the ICJ in 1959, the Cambodian government requested the ICJ to make a ruling on the following points:[7]

1. To adjudge and declare that the map of the Dongrek sector (Annex I Map, see Picture 3) was drawn up and published in the name and on behalf of the Mixed Delimitation Commission set up by the Treaty of 13 February 1904, and that it "presents a treaty character" or, in other word, it is part of the treaty.
2. To adjudge and declare that the frontier line between Cambodia and Thailand is that which is marked on the Annex I Map.
3. To adjudge and declare that the temple of Preah Vihear is situated in territory under Cambodia's sovereignty.
4. To adjudge and declare that Thailand is under an obligation to withdraw the detachments of armed forces from the temple area.
5. To adjudge and declare that Thailand must return to Cambodia the properties her authorities had earlier removed from the temple.

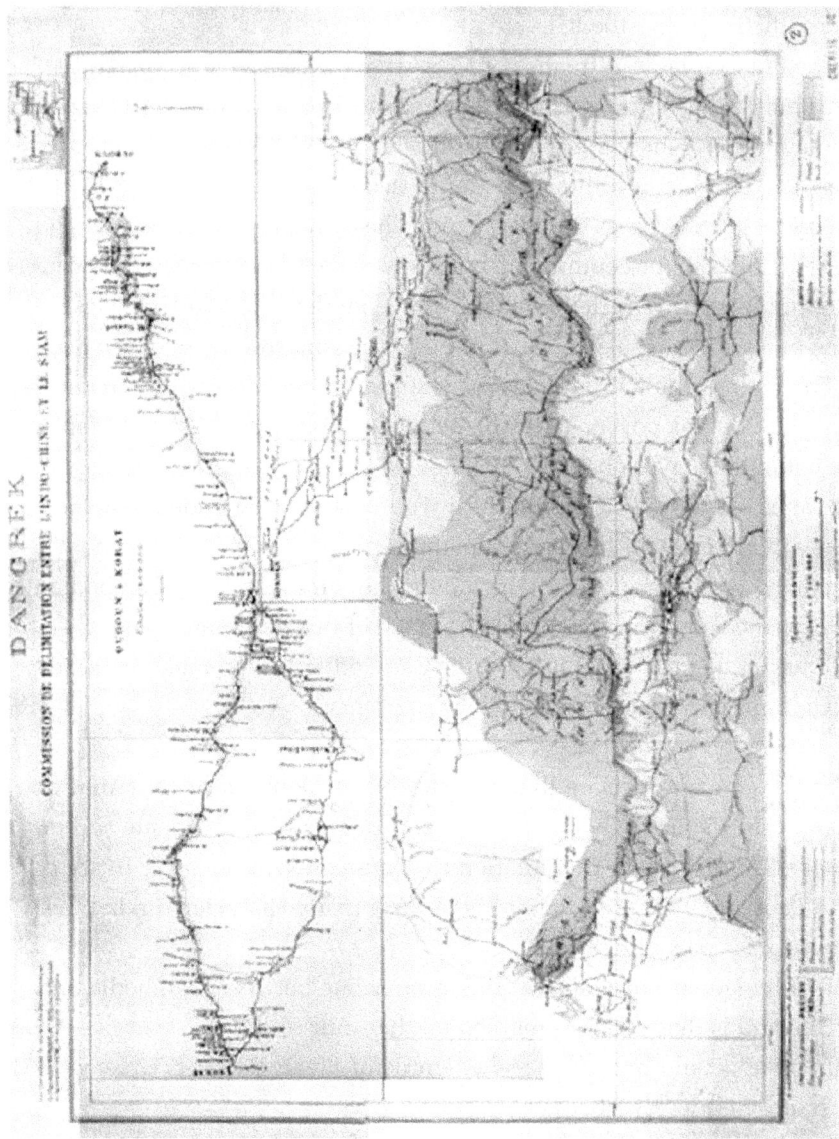

Picture 3: The Dongrek Map (Annex 1 Map), work of the Siamese-French Mixed Commission.

Thailand argued that the Annex I Map was invalid as the border line was not drawn in accordance with the watershed as stipulated in the treaties. Besides, no Siamese member had joined the Mixed Commission in the mapping work. There were only France-appointed officers in the survey team and the Annex I Map had never been formally adopted by the Commission.

To the disadvantage of Thailand, there was evidence that the Siamese government "had officially requested that the French topographical officers should map the frontier region".[8] After the mapping was complete, the French survey team sent fifty copies of the series of eleven maps to the Siamese government, who accepted the maps and distributed them to various offices both inside Siam and overseas.[9] Siam could have rejected the map if she believed that it was not the work of the Mixed Commission. But Siam did not do so, even though the map was clearly titled as "Dangrek – Commission de Délimitation entre l'Indo-Chine et le Siam" (see Picture 3).[10]

The ICJ also took into account the fact that, though years later the Thai government realized that the frontier line in the Annex I Map did not correspond to the watershed line, they apparently failed to appeal for correction despites opportunities to do so. Instead, Thai government agencies continued to use the Annex I Map which placed the Preah Vihear temple in Cambodian territory.[11] The court thus ruled that "an acknowledgement by conduct was undoubtedly made in a very definite way"[12] that "Thailand in 1908–1909 did accept the Annex I map as representing the outcome of the work of delimitation, and hence recognized the line on the map as being the frontier line, the effect of which is to situate Preah Vihear in Cambodian territory.… Both Parties, by their conduct, recognized the line and thereby in effect agreed to regard it as being the frontier line." In addition, the court considered that "the acceptance of the Annex I map by the Parties caused the map to enter the treaty settlement and to become an integral part of it".[13] The Cambodian government thus argued that the ICJ supported Cambodia's claim, and that the disputed area surrounding the temple must belong to Cambodia.

The ICJ verdict had an additional complication which opened the way to future problems. Despite its opinion about the map and the frontier line, the court declined to make any judgment on points 1 and 2 in Cambodia's request because Cambodia added these two points later. The court considered that "the subject of the dispute" was confined to "the sovereignty over the region of the temple of Preah Vihear".[14] It omitted delivering any verdict about the status of the Annex 1 Map and about the frontier line on that map. The self-contradictory nature of the court's judgment allowed Thailand to disregard the frontier line on the Annex I Map and to continue claiming that the watershed line stipulated in the 1904 and 1907 treaties was the valid frontier. Thailand thus claimed sovereignty over the area that lay between the two conflicting definitions of the border.[15] The ICJ verdict had thus failed to settle the dispute over the area around the temple.

Article 60 of the Statutes of the ICJ stipulates that the judgment is final and without appeal, and Article 61 states that no application for revision may be made after the lapse of ten years from the date of judgment.

Responsibility

Several state agencies in Thailand were involved in the decision to promote the Preah Vihear temple to World Heritage status. The Ministry of Foreign Affairs took care of diplomatic negotiation and legal matters; the Ministry of Culture oversaw the proposal to UNESCO as well as providing Cambodia with technical assistance about World Heritage conservation and management; the Ministry of Defence was in charge of protecting Thai sovereignty along the border; the Ministry of Natural Resources and Environment represented Thailand in meetings of the World Heritage Committee (WHC) and coordinated with the WHC; the National Security Council oversaw the security issue; and the Royal Survey Department surveyed border areas and carried out mapping.[16]

The Beginning of Cooperation: Tourism

Tourism has been a vital source of foreign revenue for Thailand for decades. The end of conflict in Indochina brought opportunities for Thailand to expand her tourism industry to cover long-abandoned tourist attractions in neighbouring countries. With its own well-developed tourist industry, facilities for training, and geographical proximity, Thailand aimed to become a gateway for tourism to neighbouring countries.

For war-torn Cambodia, tourism promised to be a fast way to earn foreign exchange, increase tax income, and create direct and indirect employment opportunities in various sectors. The Asian Development Bank (ADB) designated tourism development as a priority sector for poverty reduction and regional integration in the Greater Mekong Sub-region. As early as 1993, the ADB promoted tourism cooperation among GMS governments by establishing a tourism sector working group with senior representatives of national tourism organisations. The aim was to promote the sub-region as a single tourism destination. Other international organizations, such as the United Nations Economic and Social Commission for Asia and the Pacific (UNESCAP) and the United Nations Education Scientific and Cultural Organisation (UNESCO), also promoted tourism.[17]

Since the 1990s, Cambodia enjoyed increasing revenue from tourism. In 2008, tourist arrivals amounted to 2,125,465 persons and brought in revenue of US$1,596 million, 9 per cent of GDP.[18] Ten years earlier, less than 300,000 tourists had visited the country (see Table 10). Although Cambodia has many natural and cultural heritages sites, Angkor Wat has drawn the vast majority of foreign visitors (see Table 11). Angkor Wat has not only contributed significantly to Cambodia's economy, but is also a source of pride, recalling a great empire which contrasts with the current status of the country in the wake of recent wars. In September 1997, the Cambodian government launched a tourism campaign entitled "Seeing is Believing", meaning that visitors had to come and see for themselves that Cambodia was a safe place to visit.[19] Promoting cultural tourism has been a major focus of government policy since the beginning of the 1990s. One objective of that policy has been to acquire World Heritage status for more ancient sites, including the Preah Vihear temple.

Since the time of the Chatichai government, Thailand and Cambodia have concluded several bilateral agreements on tourism promotion. The Tourism Authority of Thailand (TAT) has been especially involved in providing neighbouring countries with human resource training.[20] Following Thaksin's visit to Cambodia in June 2001, the NESDB drew up a master plan for economic cooperation between Thailand and Cambodia. The study focused on the potential for economic cooperation in the border region, including seven Thai and nine Cambodian provinces. The area was dubbed

TABLE 10
Visitor Arrivals to Cambodia, 1993–2008

Year	Number of visitors	Change (%)	Revenue (million US$)
1993	118,183	0.00	N/A
1994	176,617	49.44	N/A
1995	219,680	24.38	100
1996	260,489	18.58	118
1997	218,843	−15.99	103
1998	289,524	32.30	166
1999	367,743	27.02	190
2000	466,365	26.82	228
2001	604,919	29.71	304
2002	786,524	30.02	379
2003	701,014	−10.87	347
2004	1,055,202	50.53	578
2005	1,421,615	34.72	832
2006	1,700,041	19.59	1,049
2007	2,015,128	18.53	1,400
2008	2,125,465	5.48	1,596

Source: Ministry of Tourism, Cambodia, *Tourism Statistic Report 2008*, retrieved from <http://www.tourismcambodia.com/ftp/Cambodia_Tourism_Statistics_2008.pdf> (accessed 6 January 2011).

TABLE 11
Percentage Share of Visitor Arrivals at Destination in 2008

Visitor arrivals	2007	2008
Phnom Penh & other destinations	894,542	1,065,596
Siem Reap Province	1,120,586	1,059,870
Total	2,015,128	2,125,465

Source: Ministry of Tourism, Cambodia, *Tourism Statistic Report 2008* <http://www.tourismcambodia.com/ftp/Cambodia_Tourism_Statistics_2008.pdf> (accessed 6 January 2011).

a "Crescent of Opportunity". The plan proposed several projects such as developing Siem Reap into an international conference centre and organizing cross-border package tours, such as a trip along the historical path from Phimai in northeastern Thailand to Angkor Wat, and eco-tourism along the Thai-Cambodian coastline (Trat-Koh Kong). Another interesting proposal was development of a tourism loop along the Thailand-Cambodia-Laos border area, dubbed "The Emerald Triangle", including Ubon Ratchathani (Thailand), Preah Vihear (Cambodia), and Champassak (Laos). In addition, there was a plan to promote tourism loops covering areas of Khmer civilization in both Cambodia and Thailand such as:

- Sakaew-Siem Reap-Burirum/Surin-Banteay Meanchey
- Burirum/Surin-Sikoraphum-Sisaket/Preah Vihear-Siem Reap
- Champassak-Kampong Thom-Koh Kaer-Sisaket/Preah Vihear[21]

Both Cambodia and Thailand saw benefits in cross-border tourism cooperation. Cambodia became increasingly integrated into Thailand's plan to become a centre for regional tourism. With such increased cross-border cooperation, the issue of the border line seemed to decline in significance for Thai policy-makers. Bilateral cooperation over the Preah Vihear temple was part of this trend.

Pushing for the World Heritage Site

After Thailand lost the court battle to Cambodia in 1962, the temple issue gradually faded from public attention. But the relationship between Thailand and Cambodia continued to be bumpy. Following Washington's global policy, Thailand opposed Sihanouk's neutrality in the Cold War. When the Vietnam War flowed into Cambodia and a communist insurgency grew stronger in the countryside, the Cambodian government was unable to do much with the temple. After the Khmer Rouge regime was overthrown by Vietnamese troops in January 1979, the temple and its vicinity became a Khmer Rouge military base. The temple returned to the attention of the Thai public in April 1989, when the government of Chatichai Choonhavan held a cabinet meeting in Khon Kaen Province and a group of northeastern MP submitted a request for the cabinet to allow tourists to visit the temple in order to promote tourism in the area. The cabinet supported the idea. Three months later, the Tourism Authority of Thailand (TAT) reported to the cabinet that the government of Cambodia agreed with Thailand's proposal and was ready to open the temple for visitors. Both countries agreed to cooperate in de-mining the area as well as setting up rules and regulations for visiting the temple. The Cambodian government also agreed that, after the official opening of the temple, the TAT would be in charge of organizing the inaugural tour group. As Khmer Rouge forces were still roaming in the area, the temple was closed to visitors from time to time. Later when the Cambodian conflict ended and the Khmer Rouge forces were integrated into the Cambodian army, visits to the temple resumed. In 1996, the Thai government approved funding for developing a road leading to the temple.[22] In 1997, the Thai-Cambodian Joint Commission agreed in principle to promote tourism in the area covering the lower part of northeastern Thailand and Preah Vihear Province in Cambodia.[23]

At the beginning of the Thaksin government, a plan to have the temple entered on the World Heritage list began to take shape. Following joint meetings between the Thai and Cambodian cabinets in Siem Reap, Cambodia, and Ubon Ratchathani, Thailand, on 31 May and 1 June 2003, the two countries agreed to establish a joint committee to propose guidelines for developing the temple and its surrounding area based on mutual interest. The Thai side set up one sub-committee to draft a joint development plan and another to develop a plan for conservation and restoration. At a meeting in Bangkok on 25 March 2004, the joint committee, chaired by the Thai foreign minister Surakiart Sathirathai and the Cambodian deputy prime minister Sok Anh, agreed on some basic principles.[24]

1. The Preah Vihear temple development project would be a symbol of friendship between Thailand and Cambodia. The cooperation would be based on mutual interest.
2. The Preah Vihear temple would become part of world heritage for humanity. Technical assistance would be sought from the UNESCO after the temple was inscribed as a World Heritage site.
3. Cambodia would set up two sub-committees as Thailand did. These committees would work together to solve all major problems related to

the temple, such as the disorderly shop-houses situated near the temple ground, de-mining, and environmental problems.

4. The temple project would be developed in line with other regional cooperation frameworks, such as the ACMECS.[25]

5. Thailand and Cambodia were willing to allow others parties from international organizations and the private sector to join them in developing the area.

6. The temple development project would not affect the border demarcation between the two countries.

According to a White Paper produced by the Thai Ministry of Foreign Affairs, the Thai side appeared to understand that the listing of the temple as a World Heritage site would be done jointly by Thailand and Cambodia. But a problem arose in 2007 when Cambodia submitted a nomination to the WHC without consulting Thailand. What troubled the Thai authorities most was that the map attached to the nomination file included the disputed area as a buffer zone of the World Heritage site. A team of Thai representatives at the UNESCO meeting lodged an objection against the map on grounds that it might prejudice Thailand's claim of sovereignty over the area in the future. Allowing Cambodia to pursue the World Heritage listing without any objection from Thailand might imply that Thailand accepted the demarcation line on the map as the border between the two countries. The Thai officials also argued that the nomination should have been jointly submitted by the two countries because part of the Preah Vihear complex, including the Sa Trao pond and the most convenient access to the temple from the north, were situated in Thai territory. In addition a joint listing would allow both sides to use the disputed area as the temple's buffer and development zone, which is a requirement for a World Heritage site.

However, in talks over 2007–8, Hun Sen and Sok An rejected the idea of joint nomination on grounds that Cambodia undoubtedly had sole sovereignty over the temple, and suggested that Thailand could submit a separate nomination for areas situated in Thai territory.[26]

Cambodia's refusal to pursue joint nomination was clearly based on the fact that the temple legally belongs to Cambodia. Cambodian officials may also have perceived that Thailand harboured a desire for Cambodian territory, particularly for this cultural site. The involvement of PAD only confirmed such distrust to Cambodians. Though a joint nomination would not allow Thailand to claim sovereignty over the temple, it might have given Thailand a sense of ownership, which Cambodia did not wish to share with Thailand.

In the face of Cambodia's firm refusal, Thai state agencies appeared to play down the issue of joint nomination and focused on protecting the disputed area. Since Cambodian officials declined to make any change in the map submitted to the WHC, the Thai government, now the coup-installed government of General Surayud Julanond, lodged an objection to Cambodia's submission at the 31st session of the WHC in Christchurch, New Zealand on 28 June 2007. As a result of heavy lobbying by Thai officials, the WHC decided to postpone a decision on the temple to the 32nd session in 2008.[27]

It is important to emphasize that the objection lodged by the Surayud government was solely about the map attached to the nomination, not the listing of the temple, as the former foreign minister Nit Phiboonsongkram later claimed.[28] According to a White Paper released in June 2008 by the Thai Ministry of Foreign Affairs, during the WHC meeting in Christchurch, the Surayud government told the Cambodian government and the WHC that Thailand did not oppose the temple listing but that it was necessary for Thailand and Cambodia to work out how to manage the disputed area, which would be used as the buffer and development zone.[29] The WHC agreed with Thailand that the listing should be delayed. As the WHC recorded:

> The State Party of Cambodia and the State Party of Thailand are in full agreement that the Sacred Site of the temple of Preah Vihear has Outstanding Universal Value and must be inscribed on the World Heritage List as soon as possible. Accordingly, Cambodia and Thailand agree that Cambodia will propose the site for formal inscription on the World Heritage List at the 32nd Session of the World Heritage Committee in 2008 with the active support of Thailand.[30]

The WHC noted further that Thailand and Cambodia agreed that it was essential to strengthen conservation and management at the temple site, which required close cooperation between the two countries.[31]

In preparing to resubmit the temple nomination at the 32nd WHC meeting, Cambodia and Thailand tried to resolve their differences at various occasions and eventually the Cambodian government appeared to become more sensitive to Thailand's concern. In December 2007, the People Power Party, a reincarnation of the dissolved Thai Rak Thai Party of Thaksin, won a majority in a general election. Samak Sundaravej became prime minister and Noppadon Pattama, the former legal advisor to Thaksin, was appointed as foreign minister. The change of government did not appear to affect Thailand's position on the temple issue. At an informal meeting of ASEAN foreign ministers in Singapore on 21 February 2008, the Cambodian foreign minister Hor Num Hong assured Noppadon that the listing of the temple would not prejudice Thailand's rights in the disputed area as the listing had nothing to do with border demarcation. When Samak met Hun Sen at a GMS Summit in Vientiane, the Thai side proposed that Thailand and Cambodia should work on a joint management plan for the area surrounding the temple. Hun Sen responded by saying that Cambodia was well aware that Thailand also claimed part of the surrounding area and had decided to propose listing of the temple building only; consideration of the buffer zone had thus been deleted from the nomination file. This adjustment excluded the disputed area from the map attached to the nomination file (see Picture 4). Cambodia also agreed to Thailand's idea of a joint management plan for the temple.[32]

According to the Cambodian government document *"The temple of Preah Vihear Inscribed on the World Heritage List (UNESCO) since 2008"*, the perimeter of the area in the proposal made to the WHC at the 32nd session in 2008 was revised from the version a year earlier. The agreed and finalized area was as followed:

The updated dossier presented *this property (zone 1)* covering **11** (eleven) hectares only, but the Decision of the Committee at the 31st session, announcing the process for inscription in progress, was based on the proposition of the inscription of the "**Sacred Site of**

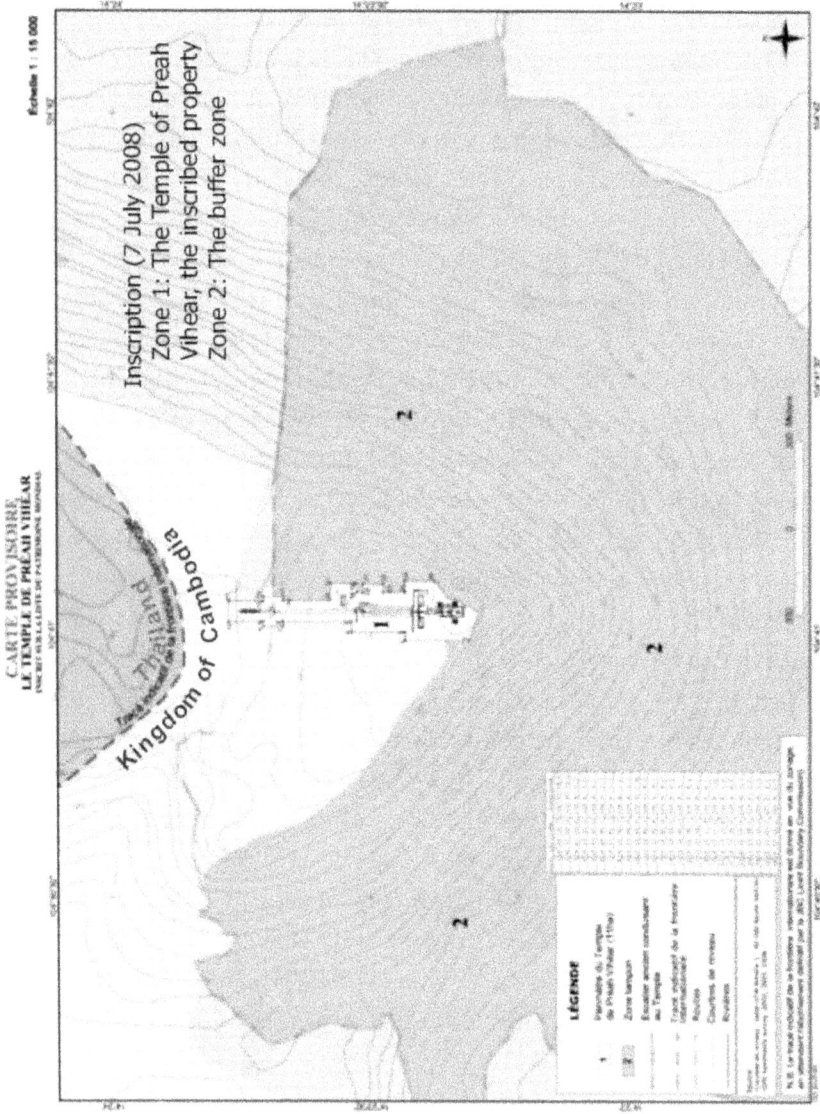

CARTE PROVISOIRE
LE TEMPLE DE PRÉAH VIHÉAR
INSCRIT SUR LA LISTE DE PATRIMOINE MONDIAL

Echelle 1 : 15 000

Inscription (7 July 2008)
Zone 1: The Temple of Preah
Vihear, the inscribed property
Zone 2: The buffer zone

Thailand

Kingdom of Cambodia

Picture 4: Map of property listed on the World Heritage list by Cambodia in 2008.
Source: Office of the Council of Ministers, Cambodia. *The Temple of Preah Vihear Inscribed on the World Heritage List (UNESCO) since 2008,* p. 34. Phnom Penh, 2010.

the temple of Preah Vihear" covering **154.70 ha (one hundred fifty four hectares and seventy acres)**.

The *buffer zone (zone 2)* identified in the RGPP (Revised Graphic Plan of the Property) as what has been accepted by the Committee at its 32nd session covers only **644.113 ha (six hundred forty four hectares and one hundred thirteen acres)**, instead of the initial buffer zone covering **2,642.50 ha (two thousand six hundred forty two hectares and fifty acres)**, when the World Heritage Committee made the Decision announcing the process for inscription in progress.[33] (See picture 4 for map of listed property).

The Cambodian government had agreed to work with Thailand in revising the map before Cambodia resubmitted the nomination to the 32nd WHC session. The revised map was examined to the satisfaction of Thailand's Royal Survey Department, the Department of Treaty and Legal Affairs of Ministry of Foreign Affairs, and the National Security Council. They all agreed that it did not include any part of the disputed area.[34]

The army chief General Anuphong Phaochinda said that "we must accept that according to the ICJ decision, the temple building belongs to Cambodia since 1962. Now Cambodia has proposed to list the temple on the World Heritage List, I do not see how Thailand would lose territory."[35] General Songkitti Chakrabat, the army chief of staff, added that "the Army would never allow any country to use our territory. We had examined both on the land and from the satellite and can confirm that we will protect our sovereignty. We did not try to protect anyone but just want to confirm the accuracy."[36] According to the director of the Royal Survey Department, Major General Daen Meechu-at, "after surveying the area, I confirm that no part of the map, which was attached to Cambodia's submission to list the temple, overlaps with the area claimed by Thailand". The Supreme Commander General Boonsang Niempradit reiterated that "the Army confirms that the map that Cambodia attached to the temple nomination does not encroach on Thai territory".[37] The good teamwork between the Foreign Ministry and the security agencies to resolve this problem was depicted clearly by the permanent secretary at the Ministry of Foreign Affairs, Virasakdi Futrakul:

The success of negotiation (with Cambodia) is partly attributed to the military, which has coordinated well with the Cambodian military. The teamwork can be described as "an iron fist in the velvet glove". That is the Ministry of Foreign Affairs and the military worked hand in hand. The military was like an iron fist while the Ministry was comparable to the velvet glove. We share the same opinion. The country's security agencies, including the Ministry of Foreign Affairs, the military, and the National Security Council, worked constantly and meticulously in order to protect Thailand's sovereignty in accordance with international laws. Whether Cambodia would succeed in listing the Preah Vihear temple on the World Heritage List, there is no worry that it would have any effect on the overlapping claimed area or the border demarcation between the two countries, because only the Thai-Cambodian Joint Border Committee has authority to decide the matter.[38]

The conclusion thus led to a Joint Communiqué supporting inscription of the temple on the World Heritage List. The Communiqué was signed by Sok Anh and Noppadon Pattama on 18 June 2008 and submitted to the WHC. Its content clearly shows flexibility and mutual conciliation between the officials of both countries. Some of the noteworthy points are:

Thailand supports the inscription of the temple of Preah Vihear on the World Heritage List proposed by Cambodia …

In the spirit of goodwill and conciliation, Cambodia accepts that the temple be nominated for inscription *without at this stage a buffer zone on the northern and western areas of the temple*. Only the buffer zone of the eastern and southern areas of the temple are maintained …

Pending the work of the Joint Commission for Land Boundary concerning the northern and western areas of the temple, *the management plan of the northern and western areas surrounding the temple will be prepared in a concerted manner between Thailand and Cambodia*. Such management plan will be included in the final management plan for the temple and its surrounding areas to be submitted to the WHC by 1st February 2010 …

The inscription of the temple shall be without prejudice to the rights of the Cambodia and Thailand on the demarcation works of the Joint Commission for Land Boundary of the two countries.[39]

Finally, the WHC granted the Preah Vihear temple the status of a World Heritage site on 7 July 2008.

Summary

Bilateral cooperation over the Preah Vihear temple was a multi-dimensional issue between Thailand and Cambodia. It was not only about territorial sovereignty.

Through the 1950s and 1960s, the issue of sovereignty over the temple of Preah Vihear had damaged the relationship between Thailand and Cambodia, but by the 1990s the memory of the ICJ decision awarding the temple to Cambodia did not appear to have any lingering sentimental effect on the Thai state agencies involved with the temple issue. Local business people, the Tourism Authority of Thailand, and other governmental agencies were more interested in how to turn the ancient ruin into business profit with full acknowledgement that the temple and the territory on which it stands legitimately belonged to Cambodia. Creating economic prosperity was clearly the leading consideration in post-Cold War relations between Thailand and Cambodia. Thailand's support for Cambodia's nomination of the temple as a World Heritage site originated from this framework. Cooperation to develop tourism at Preah Vihear temple was in line with Thailand's policy to position itself as a regional centre. Moreover, the inscription of the temple on the World Heritage list was also based on the mutual objective of turning the once disputed monument into a symbol of friendship and cooperation between Thailand and Cambodia. This commendable objective shows that the Thai state agencies' decision making was not shaped by any bitter memory of past defeat. On the contrary, as discussed in Chapter II, Thai state agencies were aware that people in neighbouring countries held negative attitudes toward Thailand, which could affect Thailand's long-term interest in the region, and that Thailand needed to demonstrate goodwill and conciliation toward these neighbours. The cultivation of goodwill had become an important part of the policy of post-Cold War Thai governments, long before Thaksin became prime minister. The support for the temple's listing given by the successive governments of Thaksin, Surayud, and Samak was part of this strategy. Though historical distrust resulted in Cambodia's refusal to go ahead with a joint nomination, the Thai side showed great flexibility and goodwill in continuing to support the nomination, provided that the nomination did not affect the issue of sovereignty over the disputed area. In return, the Cambodian government became more understanding of the Thai government's concern and agreed to change the map attached to the nomination so that it no longer included the disputed area in the map. Significantly, when it was clear that establishing sole sovereignty over the area surrounding the temple was not possible, at least for the time being, both sides agreed to the idea of a joint development plan for the area. The negotiation thus displayed a serious attempt by Thai and Cambodian officials to solve a sensitive territorial dispute by cultural and economic means. This initiative should have been encouraged and appreciated. Unfortunately, while government-to-government negotiations were leading in a positive direction, Thai domestic politics were not. The long-standing bilateral cooperation regarding the Preah Vihear temple and its surrounding area collapsed when Thai politics headed into a crisis and the nationalist drum started beating relentlessly.

Notes

1. Office of Archaeology, Fine Arts Department, Ministry of Culture and ICOMOS, Thailand, *Management Plan for Preah Vihear Mountain and Its Setting* (Bangkok, 2008), p. 4.
2. International Court of Justice (hereafter ICJ), *Reports of Judgments, Advisory Opinions and Orders, Case Concerning the temple of Preah Vihear (Cambodia v. Thailand), Judgment of 15 June 1962* (1962), pp. 31–32.
3. ICJ, *Case Concerning the temple of Preah Vihear*, pp. 36–37.
4. Charnvit Kasetsiri, *Latthi chatniyom thai/sayam kap kamphucha: lae korani sueksa prasat khaophrawihan* [Siamese/Thai nationalism and Cambodia: A case study of the Preah Vihear temple] (Bangkok: Foundation of the Promotion of the Social Science and Humanities Books Project, 2009), p. 137.
5. For further discussion of the implication of the memory of lost territories for Thai nationalism and nation-state formation, see Thongchai Winichakul, *Siam Mapped: A History of the Geo-body of a Nation* (Honolulu: University of Hawaii Press, 1994).

6. Ministry of Foreign Affairs, Thailand, (hereafter MFA), *Korani kankhuen thabian prasat phrawihan pen moradok lok* [The Inscription of the temple of Preah Vihear on the World Heritage List] (Bangkok: June 2008), pp. 26–28.
7. ICJ, *Case concerning the temple of Preah Vihear*, p. 11.
8. Ibid., p. 20.
9. Ibid., pp. 23, 29.
10. Ibid., p. 24.
11. Ibid., pp. 25–29.
12. Ibid., p. 23.
13. Ibid., pp. 32–33.
14. Ibid., p. 14.
15. MFA, Thailand, *The Inscription of the temple of Preah Vihear*, p. 2.
16. Ibid., p. 8.
17. Asian Development Bank (hereafter ADB), *Technical Assistance to the Mekong/ Lancang River Tourism Planning Study* (June 1997) <www.adb.org/Documents/ TARs/REG/30015-STU-TAR.pdf> (accessed 6 January 2011).
18. Ministry of Tourism, Cambodia, *Cambodia, Tourism Statistical Report 2008* (Phnom Penh, n.d.) <http://www.tourismcambodia.com/ftp/Cambodia_Tourism_ Statistics_2008.pdf> (accessed 6 January 2011).
19. Watcharin Yongsiri, *Border Trade*, pp. 166–67.
20. MFA, Thailand, *The Foreign Ministry's Work Between 1997–2000* (Bangkok: n.d.), p. 53; University of Thai Chamber of Commerce, *Study on Investment Promotion in Laos, Cambodia and Myanmar* (Bangkok: 2004), pp. 4-7 – 4-8.
21. Thailand Institute of Scientific and Technological Research, *Krongkan jat tham phaen patibatkan phatthana samliam thongthieo chuemyong thai lao kamphucha* [Operational plan for developing the tourism triangle between Thailand, Laos, and Cambodia] Report submitted to Tourism Authority of Thailand, (Bangkok:1999), 8-6, 8-18.
22. Bavornsak Uwanno, *Chae ekkasanlap thisut prasat phrawihan pho.so.2505-2551* [Disclosing the highly confidential documents, the temple of Preah Vihear 1962–2008] (Bangkok: Matichon Publications, 2008), pp. 253–54.
23. MFA, Thailand, *The Inscription of the temple of Preah Vihear*, p. 40.
24. Bavornsak Uwanno, *Disclosing the Highly Confidential Documents*, pp, 254–55.
25. ACMECS is a cooperation framework amongst Cambodia, Lao PDR, Myanmar, Thailand and Vietnam to promote cooperation and development in the sub-region. It was initiated by Thaksin Shinawatra in April 2003 with an intention to replace the Greater Mekong Sub-region framework. However, the objectives and policies of ACMECS are not much different from the GMS while many GMS programmes are still in operation. One of the ACMECS's new flagship programmes was the cross-border contract farming programme.

26. MFA, Thailand, *The Inscription of the temple of Preah Vihear*, pp. 4–5.

27. Ibid., p. 10; Bavornsak Uwannao, *Disclosing the Highly Confidential Documents*, pp. 254–55.

28. An attempt to distance the Surayud government from the temple listing took place during the peak of the PAD's campaign against the Samak government.

29. MFA, Thailand, *The Inscription of the temple of Preah Vihear*, pp. 9–10.

30. World Heritage Committee (hereafter WHC), *The 31st session of the Committee — Christchurch, New Zealand — July 2007. Decision No 31 COM 8B.24*.

31. Ibid.

32. MFA, Thailand, *The Inscription of the temple of Preah Vihear*, pp. 11–12.

33. The Office of the Council of Ministers, Cambodia, *The temple of Preah Vihear Inscribed on the World Heritage List (UNESCO) since 2008* (Phnom Penh, 2010), p. 28. Emphasis in original.

34. MFA, Thailand, *The Inscription of the temple of Preah Vihear*, pp. 12–13; Bavornsak Uwanno, *The Highly Declassified Documents*, pp. 264–65.

35. "Noppadol topkratu so.wo. o penphujeraja maihai thai siangsiadindaen" [Noppadol responses to senators, claims to prevent Thailand from territorial loss], *Matichon*, 19 June 2008.

36. "Kongthap karanti mai sia dindaen khuenthabian khaophrawihan moradoklok" [The army guarantees the temple listing will cause no territorial loss], *Thairath*, 19 June 2008.

37. Statements by Daen and Boonsang are quoted from MFA, Thailand, *The Inscription of the temple of Preah Vihear*, pp. cho-so.

38. Quoted from MFA, Thailand, *The Inscription of the temple of Preah Vihear*, p. cho.

39. Joint Communiqué between Thailand and Cambodia, signed on 18 June 2008, italics added.

CHAPTER IV

Uncivil Society in Polarized Politics

This chapter will discuss the campaign of the People's Alliance for Democracy (PAD) over the Preah Vihear temple and will analyse factors contributing to its success. It is true that PAD has been able to manipulate the bitter history of Thailand's past territorial losses as a powerful tool in its campaign, as several scholars have pointed out.[1] This study will, therefore, not repeat that issue. I would like to argue that while nationalist history is indeed a crucial factor in the temple conflict, we need to take into consideration the roles of several actors, both state and non-state, in legitimizing the PAD's campaign on the temple issue. These actors, which included academics, former diplomats, independent organizations such as the National Human Rights Commission, the Administrative Court, the Constitution Court, and the media, were considered authoritative, pro-democracy, impartial, and independent. Therefore, their support gave both moral and legal legitimacy to the PAD's temple campaign.

PAD and Its Allies

PAD was a coalition of heterogeneous groups with diverse and even conflicting backgrounds and interests. What united these diverse groups was their opposition to Thaksin. The alliance can be divided into two major strands. One was a network of grassroots and mass-based civil society organizations, such as the Alternative Agriculture Network, Northern Farmers Alliance, and Southern Federation of Small Scale Fishermen, along with state enterprise labour unions which opposed Thaksin's privatization policy and various NGOs involved in issues of consumer protection, anti-privatization, human rights, environmental protection, anti-free trade policy, communitarian development, and pro-democracy issues. This wing included many who had been strong supporters of Thaksin during the early years of the Thai Rak Thai Party (TRT). Many civil society leaders participated in developing the TRT's policies, and helped connect the party with the masses in rural and urban areas, especially in the north and northeast. They saw Thaksin as a champion who could rescue Thailand from the forces of Western dominated globalization, which had taken advantage of the 1997 economic crisis to loot Thailand's resources and crush the country's pride, particularly through the IMF bailout package. Many rural development NGO leaders also believed that the TRT policies were pro-poor, anti-neo-liberalism, and empowering for local communities. But the activists and leaders of most civil society organizations fell out with Thaksin after he became prime minister and increasingly confident of his popularity so that he no longer needed to depend on their support. Thaksin started to criticize NGOs leaders and activists as trouble-makers while pursuing neo-liberal policies to privatize state enterprises and conclude free trade agreements with various foreign countries. These policies were seen as benefiting Thaksin's own business empire and his patronage network while having an immense negative impact on the livelihood of the poor. Furthermore, the appalling violence that resulted from government policy in the Muslim-dominated south and during the government's "war on drugs" drew opposition from human rights groups.[2] While many NGOs leaders and intellectuals divorced themselves from Thaksin and the TRT, the majority of the rural mass still supported Thaksin because of his pro-poor policy. They later became supporters of the Red Shirt movement.

The second strand of PAD was dominated by two ultra royalist, conservative, and nationalist leaders, Sondhi Limthongkul and retired Major General Chamlong Srimuang. Sondhi was a media mogul, head of the Manager Media group. He had been a business associate of Thaksin but had fallen out with him over a business deal. Sondhi drew support from the urban and conservative elite, including royalist civil servants and business groups that were not part of Thaksin's patronage network and thus felt excluded from attractive business opportunities. Chamlong Srimuang had been leader of the May 1992 anti-military uprising, and was a lay leader of the "Dharma Army", part of Santi Asoke, a radical Buddhist sect headed by Phra Bodirak, who had declared independence from the Ecclesiastical Council in 1975. Members of the Dharma Army were among the most fervent supporters of PAD. This wing of PAD had adopted the colour yellow as their uniform because of its association with the king, leading to the popular dubbing of PAD as the "Yellow Shirts". Middle class urbanites formed the majority of the Yellow Shirt mass. As Chamlong and Sondhi were the most influential leaders, the loyalist conservative force eventually dominated the PAD movement.[3]

PAD claimed that its objective was to clean up corruption in Thai politics and to restore full democracy, which had been severely crippled during the six years of Thaksin's government. But their actions, demands, rationale, and discourse ran athwart what they claimed to be. The PAD played a significant role in the politics leading to the 2006 coup which Thongchai Winichakul described as a collaboration among the palace, royalists, people's sector, NGO activists, and intellectuals to undermine electoral democracy. PAD supporters perceived the unprecedented popularity of a politician like Thaksin as a challenge to the shadowy dominant power of the king. In Thongchai's view, the anti-Thaksin coalition's claim to achieve "clean politics" was simply the latest effort by royalists to take control of the country's democratization process.[4] After the coup, the palace, military and bureaucracy resumed a guardian role over the legislature — something that the 1997 Constitution had removed. Repressive laws and media controls were used to stifle the pro-Thaksin groups. The Yellow Shirts movement revived a highly royalist, conservative, and nationalist discourse against not only Thaksin and his supporters but also any independent media and intellectuals who challenged their propaganda and political agenda. After the coup, Thai politics became deeply polarized as the PAD, royalists, military and bureaucracy tried to consolidate their dominant position, disregarding the results of popular elections and the rule of law.[5] The PAD's campaign over the temple of Preah Vihear was an attempt to exploit deep-rooted nationalism against the pro-Thaksin faction and against Cambodia.

The overthrow of Thaksin's government by a military coup in 2006 only rendered the anti-Thaksin force a temporary victory since electoral support for Thaksin remained strong, especially in the northern and northeastern regions. In December 2007, the PPP won a majority in the general election, and Samak Sundaravej, a veteran right-wing politician, became prime minister. In February 2008, PAD declared that it was opposed to the Samak government because it was Thaksin's proxy and would try to restore Thaksin's power and promote his interests. The PAD's primary objective was to topple the Samak government. In May 2008 when Samak announced plans to amend the 2007 constitution written during the post-coup regime, PAD launched street rallies accusing Samak of seeking to re-establish the power of political parties at the expense of independent institutions. Samak lowered the political temperature by referring the constitutional amendment to a parliamentary committee, and PAD failed to mobilize enough mass support to threaten Samak's administration, in part because the government had not been in office long enough to have any track record, and in part because the issue was not attention-grabbing.

A new opportunity emerged for PAD when the governments of Cambodia and Thailand prepared to nominate Preah Vihear temple as a World Heritage site. News about the nomination appeared from March 2008 but did not draw much attention from the Thai public until PAD took up the issue to campaign against the Samak government.[6]

Lost Territories

During the 1962 court battle and its aftermath, the size of the area that was claimed by both sides was not quantified. Only when the issue re-emerged in mid-2008 was the disputed area defined as "4.6 square kilometres". This figure was reached by comparing the Dongrek/Annex I map against a map in the L7017/7018 series of maps covering the whole of Thailand produced with assistance from a U.S. military survey team during the Cold War period.[7] It is not clear who invented this phrase or even whether the measurement is accurate, but PAD enthusiastically adopted the phrase and succeeded in making it a prominent part of the public debate. This measurement of the disputed area somehow made it more concrete, and its loss more critical.

Since the conflict over the temple emerged in early 2008, several books have appeared on the subject, written by both professional academics and others, and sharing a similar pattern.[8] As historical background to the conflict, these books describe how Thailand was unjustly forced to give up a huge amount of territory to the British and French colonial powers in order to maintain her independence and sovereignty; the most traumatic loss was France's take-over of Laos and Cambodia; the loss of the Preah Vihear temple in the 1962 court battle was a legacy of a wicked plan by the French demarcation team, which allowed Cambodia to inherit what should have belonged to Thailand.

Many generations of Thai students have studied from history textbooks that dwell on the traumatic memory of territorial loss. The fallacy of this historical narrative, or what Thongchai Winichakul terms "a royal nationalist historiography", is that it projects the notion of a modern nation-state with fixed boundaries back into the era of traditional Southeast Asian polities.[9] The nationalist version cannot accept or comprehend the idea that pre-colonial Southeast Asian states had no fixed boundaries and that inter-state relations were loose and flexible, depended on the flux of power relations.

The older versions of this history of losing territories, as written by various scholars and reproduced many times since the 1940s, did not include the case of the Preah Vihear temple. But the current sixth-grade history textbook includes the story of the ICJ case as another loss. While earlier version listed only eight occasions of loss, the current textbook inflates the number to fourteen.[10]

Professor Sompong Sucharitkul, an academic associated with PAD, argued that the Samak government's endorsement of the World Heritage listing would result in Thailand losing the right to recover the temple. He added that Thailand had never accepted the ICJ verdict, in fact had never accepted Cambodia' sovereignty over the temple, because Thailand had not recognized the 1908 map drawn by the Mixed Commission of Siam and France.[11] Sompong told the Thai media that Thailand still had the right to appeal the 1962 verdict of the ICJ. Sompong is a retired diplomat, now dean of a law faculty at a private university in Bangkok, and once part of the Thai legal team in the 1962 court battle. With these credentials, his misinformation was uncritically embraced by the Thai media. PAD reiterated that Thailand still had a right to reclaim the temple, even though Article 60 of the ICJ's Statute clearly stipulates that the judgment is final and without appeal and Article 61 adds that no application for revision may be made after the lapse of ten years from the date of the judgment. In the last 46 years, Thailand has never made any attempt to revise the case with the ICJ.

Along with Professor Adul Wichiencharoen, a retired history professor and former head of the Thailand World Heritage Committee, Sompong insisted that, had Cambodia succeeded in listing the temple, Thailand would have lost more territory to Cambodia just as it had lost Battambang and Siemreap to the French in 1907. The WHC requires that every site nominated for inclusion as World Heritage have a buffer zone defined in the nomination. The PAD academics asserted that Cambodia deliberately included the disputed area as the buffer zone, and that the Samak government' support for the nomination would have resulted in the loss of this territory.[12] Professor Srisak Vallibhodom, a highly respected expert in anthropology and archaeology, claimed that by this endorsement of the temple listing "Thailand was paying for its foolishness for the third time!" Srisak explained that the first act of foolishness was being cheated by the boundary mapping of the French Commission, and the second was the ICJ verdict in 1962.[13] Srisak publicly encouraged PAD to lead its Yellow Shirt followers to occupy the temple on grounds that only patriotic Thais could reclaim the temple because the government was unreliable.[14]

It is true that a buffer zone is required for a World Heritage site but no part of the disputed area was included in the temple's buffer zone. As explained in Chapter III, the Cambodian government agreed to exclude the disputed area from the final nomination file. Only areas on the eastern and southern sides of the temple were designated as the buffer zone. PAD's academics simply disregarded this fact. Instead of giving credit to Noppadon Pattama, who had led the team which negotiated this exclusion, Adul cast suspicion on him, alleging there might be a secret deal that motivated Cambodia to agree to the Samak government's demand so easily.[15] However, Samak had made a strategic mistake in appointing Noppadon as foreign minister because Noppadon's close link with Thaksin opened the way for allegations that he was working to protect his former boss' interest rather than the national interest. It made the accusation of "selling out the motherland" seem credible for the anti-Thaksin mass. Noppadon was the main target of a no-confidence debate led by the Democrat party on 25 June 2008. The debate was held in parallel with a PAD street rally attacking the government's policy on the temple listing. Among the seven cabinet members targeted in the debate, Noppadon received the lowest number of supporting votes. Even some coalition MPs did not vote for him.[16] Another blow to Noppadon came when the Constitution Court ruled that the Joint Communiqué with Cambodia, signed by Noppadon and Cambodian deputy prime minister Sok Anh, had violated the Constitution's Article 190 because it needed approval from parliament.[17] Noppadon was pressured to resign on 10 July 2008.

After Noppadon had resigned, Samak asked a veteran diplomat Tej Bunnag to be foreign minister. Samak hoped that Tej's reputation as an experienced and honest diplomat would counter the PAD's accusations against his government. But Tej resigned after only 39 days in office, explaining in interview that he and his family were unable to stand the pressure, and he feared being labelled as a traitor for selling the nation.[18]

PAD made Thaksin's conflict of interest over the temple listing a dominant theme of their campaign. *ASTV Manager Online*, the PAD mouthpiece, alleged that Thaksin wanted to secure a concession for offshore oil exploration and development for PTT Exploration and Production PCL (PTTEP), a Thai public company.[19] Academics such as Srisak, Thepmontri Limpaphayom, and Wanwipha Charoonroj, a researcher at Thammasat University, as well as former diplomats such as Kasit Piromya and Surapong Jayanama, joined in the chorus on this issue.[20] PAD also alleged that Thailand had lost its claims over some disputed maritime territory when in July 2009 Cambodia granted a concession for a French company to explore for oil and gas in this territory.[21] The Thai mainstream media repeated these allegations without investigating the matter thoroughly. In fact, Cambodia had granted concessions over the whole area to other foreign oil companies since 1991. PTTEP had gained only one concession, some time earlier in April 2005, in an area outside the disputed zone.[22] Besides, in 1997, Thailand and Cambodia had agreed not to conduct any activities in the disputed area before they had completed the demarcation of boundaries or had agreed on a plan of joint development.[23] In 2001 the two countries had signed a Memorandum of Understanding on joint development of the disputed area, but there had been no progress subsequently.[24]

In June 2008 the Thai media also reported that Thaksin was planning to invest in a casino complex in Cambodia's coastal town of Koh Kong, and speculated that the agreement over the temple was part of a deal to facilitate this investment. However, the media report provided no detail of this investment and was patently self-contradictory.[25] It alleged that Thaksin's project was still only a plan or an idea, which would have been strange given that Thailand and Cambodia had agreed in principle since mid-2003 to pursue the listing of the temple. If the agreement on the temple was a result of Thaksin's conflict of interests, surely his business in Cambodia should have been well established by 2008. If Thaksin indeed had any plan to invest in Cambodia, there was no evidence or logic to link this matter with the temple listing.

The demarcation of land boundaries and maritime boundaries between Thailand and Cambodia are totally different issues with different laws and documentation. Since 1968, Thailand had granted concessions to several transnational oil companies to explore in the disputed area, while Cambodia had also started to grant concessions in 1991. However, these concessions were issued solely with the aim of staking out claims to sovereignty. Actual exploration and extraction of natural resources in these zones cannot start until the two countries agree a plan for joint development of the area.[26] This fact was deliberately omitted from the PAD's propaganda. They fed their followers with half truths and blatant falsehoods. As a result, PAD's followers interpreted the inclusion of the temple on the World Heritage list as a national disaster. Srisak accused the WHC and Cambodian government of colluding to the detriment of Thailand's interests.[27]

Combating Misinformation

A small group of academics, led by the highly respected historian Charnvit Kasetsiri, has long been devoted to improving the Thai public's understanding of its Southeast Asian neighbours.[28] Charnvit and others, including myself, tried to warn the public of the danger of ultra-nationalism, prejudice, and misleading information. The group organized many open forums at various universities both in Bangkok and upcountry and also published booklets and articles about the temple issues. Charnvit's position as secretary of the Foundation for the Promotion of Social Science and Humanities Textbooks Project gave him an opportunity to educate the Thai public on Southeast Asian issues by producing many publications on Southeast Asia. For example, at the 2009 annual conference of the Foundation, Charnvit launched three books on Thai-Cambodian relations.[29] Charnvit's group gained little attention and space in the mainstream media, while the nationalist viewpoint appeared regularly and often on mainstream TV, radio, press and electronic media. Over time the minority view has started to gain more space in the media, but is still far from being able to challenge the dominant nationalist view that the media has continually presented to the public.

Moreover, PAD attacked Charnvit's group, using tactics of character assassination, painting them as traitorous scholars who sold their motherland, who accepted bribes from Thaksin, and who were Thais with Khmer minds.[30] Srisak said in interview:

> I want to ask if there is any chauvinism in Thailand. No, there is no such thing. It was an invention. Thai people just love their motherland. They will not allow the loss of territory. That is not chauvinism. That is patriotism, which is in every human being's conscience .... There is no nationalism, nor chauvinism among Thai people. There are only those who love their nation and those who betray their nation (*khai chat*). I dare to declare that I love my nation, my motherland.[31]

Sources of PAD Support

The mainstream media ferociously lashed out at Cambodia and its leader Hun Sen as the cause of conflict. With no apparent awareness of the irony, they blamed Hun Sen for trying to stir up nationalism by exploiting the temple listing to mobilize mass popularity against Thailand. The nomination of the temple at the WHC in Quebec on 2–10 July 2008 happened to come about three weeks before a Cambodian general election on 27 July. The Thai media portrayed the dispute over the temple as a tactic by Hun Sen's

Cambodian People's Party to win electoral support.[32] Thai nationalists could not accept that PAD had triggered the conflict and that their opposition to the listing had provided Hun Sen with the opportunity to play the nationalist card. They seemed to have little conception of the depth and stability of Hun Sen's power. The 2008 election was certainly not his first victory, nor the last. The temple dispute with Thailand and the inclusion on the World Heritage list may have helped increase his popularity but it was not a decisive factor in his victory. Since 1993, he had built his political empire through economic policies as well as political manipulation. Ironically, by hating Hun Sen so much, the Thai nationalists helped him to increase his popularity and his power. The temple issue unified Cambodians behind Hun Sen in his conflict with Thailand.[33]

The mainstream media continued to insult and demonize Hun Sen, especially when he invited Thaksin to become his economic advisor and refused to extradite Thaksin back to Thailand.[34] An editorial in the *Khom Chad Luek* daily condemned Hun Sen for his arrogance toward Thailand, disregarding the relations between the two countries and international law, portraying Hun Sen as a tyrant who led Vietnamese troops to invade Cambodia and massacre his own people. The writer even stated wishfully that the conflict with Thailand over the temple would lead to unrest in Cambodia and the overthrow of Hun Sen.[35] Another column in the same newspaper lambasted Hun Sen as a corrupt leader who sold his own country's natural resources to foreign investors. The columnist asserted that 40 per cent of Cambodia was sold to foreigners already. Though the content of the column was aimed at Hun Sen, its title "Cambodia…the nation for sale?" was intended to denigrate the country.[36]

While in power from 2001 to 2006, Thaksin had made a bad mistake in antagonizing the media. Though he built widespread popular support among the rural population and urban poor, his intolerance of criticism resulted in attempts to interfere and dominate the media in several forms, including buying shares in a public television channel, pursuing defamation charges against journalists, cutting state advertisements, and even issuing threats to media personnel.[37] By the end of his rule, the media orchestrated attacks on Thaksin and his proxies in the hope of preventing his return to power.

The Preah Vihear temple issue became part of the media's campaigning to delegitimize Thaksin and his party.

The PAD's nationalist campaign on the temple also received a boost from supposedly independent organizations such as the National Human Rights Commission (NHRC). Soon after the WHC approved the temple listing, the NHRC and a group of Thai senators sent letters of protest to the UN secretary-general Ban Ki-Moon, the director of UNESCO, the director and members of the WHC, the UN Human Rights High Commissioner, the UN Regional Human Rights Commissioner, and the members of the International Council on Monuments and Sites (ICOMOS). The letters accused the WHC of aggravating Thai-Cambodian relations and violating the Thai people's human rights because the listing provoked armed clashes between the two countries and loss of life. The letters demanded that Ban Ki-Moon investigate the conduct of the WHC.[38]

The NHRC's role in the conflict over Preah Vihear was rather surprising because it is hard to claim that the case involved any violation of human rights principles. In the recent past, Thaksin had antagonized human rights advocates who accused him of serious violation of human rights in his "war on drugs" and his heavy handed policy in the three southernmost Muslim-majority provinces. In response to a journalist's question on the day after the 2006 coup, the chairman of the NHRC at the time, Professor Saneh Chammarik, justified the coup as a necessary step to solve the country's political crisis. In a separate interview, Saneh clarified that "the coup is the only viable option left. Don't look at it as a step backward because we had reached the most backward point. The constitution was cornered (by Thaksin). I myself do not see the coup as a step backward or forward but a resolution to the situation." Saneh voiced his support for the Yellow Shirt movement and his suspicion of the Red Shirts. He believed that "the People's Alliance for Democracy's political activities helped arouse people political consciousness but may be using methods that some may not agree with. That is still debatable. However, this group reflects a social reaction against the Thaksin regime. Then, there is the pro-Thaksin group, which tried to cause trouble and led to confrontation."[39] A strong desire to have Thaksin removed from power led the NHRC chairman to abandon the principles of democracy and civil rights.

The Administrative Court and Constitution Court, both of which were established by the 1997 constitution, also seemed to side with the anti-Thaksin movement. On 24 June 2008, PAD petitioned the Administrative Court to suspend the Thai-Cambodian Joint Communiqué on the listing of the temple. Four days later, the Court issued an injunction, ordering the cabinet to temporarily suspend the Joint Communiqué. Then, on 29 December, the Court ordered that the Joint Communiqué be revoked.[40] In addition, the opposition Democrat Party and a group of senators, many of them appointed after the 2006 coup, petitioned the Constitution Court to decide whether the Joint Communiqué violated the Constitution. On 8 July 2008, the Court ruled that the Joint Communiqué had indeed violated the Constitution's Article 190 as it needed approval from parliament.[41] The ruling forced Noppadon Pattama to resign as foreign minister immediately.

However, the legitimacy of these rulings was questioned. Two law professors, Bovornsak Uwanno and Worajet Pakeerat, argued that the Administrative Court had no jurisdiction over the case because the Administrative Court's jurisdiction was limited to cases involving disputes between individuals and bureaucratic organizations, while the Joint Communiqué was the work of government, which was subject to the checks and balances of the parliamentary system.[42]

Other rulings confirmed a growing perception that the judiciary was using double standards in its treatment of various political factions. After the Administrative Court had issued an injunction to suspend the Joint Communiqué, Samak's cabinet and the Ministry of Foreign Affairs submitted an appeal to the Supreme Administrative Court, which overturned the lower court's ruling in a majority decision. However, before all the five judges had signed the ruling, the chairman of the Supreme Administrative Court, Ackaratorn Chularat, ordered that the case be transferred to a new team of judges, which later upheld the ruling against the Samak administration. Ackaratorn's interference was widely perceived as politically motivated. The Counter Corruption Commission (CCC) initiated an investigation of Ackaratorn's conduct but met strong resistance from judicial circles claiming the CCC had had no jurisdiction over the judiciary.[43]

Worajet Pakeerat criticized the Constitution Court's judgment as tantamount to rewriting the Constitution. The judgment stated that the

Joint Communiqué had the character of a treaty which *may result* in altering Thailand's territory, and therefore under Article 190 Paragraph 2 of the 2007 Constitution must be approved by parliament. But Worajet argued that Article 190 clearly states that a treaty which *results* in altering the country's territory must be approved by parliament, and that the word *"may"* in the ruling indicated that the Court was unable to confirm if the Joint Communiqué resulted in any territorial change or not. The Court thus extended the scope of the law more than was allowed.[44]

When the PAD campaign to topple the Samak administration gained momentum, it received more assistance from the judiciary. On 9 September 2008, Samak resigned after the Constitution Court ruled that he had violated the Constitution by accepting payment for hosting two TV cooking programmes. When Somchai Wongsawat, Thaksin's brother-in-law, then became prime minister, PAD felt justified in continuing its campaign to uproot the influence of Thaksin and his proxies. The PAD campaign reached a new peak when several thousand Yellow Shirts stormed into Government House. After a month-long occupation failed to topple the Somchai government, PAD moved its followers to occupy Bangkok's two international airports, effectively shutting down the entire air traffic of the capital. PAD soon received another helping hand from the judiciary when the Constitution Court delivered a judgment to dissolve the People Power Party on 2 December 2008. Politicking by the military and members of the establishment then put together a new coalition headed by the Democrat Party and supported by some of the smaller parties that had been coalition partners in the Samak and Somchai governments. Abhisit Vejjajiva, head of the Democrats, became prime minister.

Since the 2006 coup, anti-Thaksin intellectuals have called for *"tulakanphiwat"*, judicialization, meaning the mobilizing of the judiciary to solve contentious political problems. The 1997 and 2007 constitutions had empowered the courts, especially the Administrative Court, the Constitution Court, and the Supreme Court's Criminal Division for Persons Holding Political Offices, to settle political cases. The anti-Thaksin forces urged the supposedly moral and impartial judges of these courts to play a courageous role in solving the country's political crisis. But a series of questionable rulings against Thaksin and his faction but in favour of the anti-Thaksin faction greatly damaged the judiciary's reputation for fairness and integrity. More people now perceived the courts as a tool of the establishment to eradicate Thaksin's power. The dubious rulings related to the Preah Vihear temple issue also attracted such criticism. The Red Shirts used the phrase "double standards" to question the bias evident in the courts' decisions on various cases. The judicialization of Thai politics became the politicisation of the Thai judiciary.

The Abhisit Government and the Preah Vihear Temple

Swept along by the tide of nationalism and anti-Thaksin sentiment, Abhisit Vejjajiva as leader of the opposition had unreservedly embraced the PAD's position on the Preah Vihear temple and its surrounding area. But when he became prime minister, this position put hurdles in the path of any attempt to solve the dispute with Cambodia. Relations with Cambodia rapidly deteriorated and Hun Sen unleashed aggressive verbal attacks against Abhisit.

During the no-confidence debate against the Samak government on 24 June 2008, Abhisit claimed that Thailand had never accepted the ICJ verdict granting the Preah Vihear temple to Cambodia. Though he acknowledged that there was a 10-year time limit on any appeal at the ICJ, Abhisit insisted that Thailand had a right to appeal the verdict. He condemned the Samak government for endorsing Cambodia's nomination of the temple on grounds it forfeited Thailand's right to reclaim the temple and caused Thailand to lose sovereignty over the disputed area surrounding the temple. He argued that the temple should belong to Thailand because access was on the Thai side. If people wanted to enter the temple from the Cambodian side, he said, they had to climb up a cliff as high as the Empire State Building.[45] Such perception was widespread among the Thai public. In fact, there were two roads linking lowland Cambodia with the eastern and western sides of the temple. These two roads had been abandoned during the civil war in Cambodia, but the government had started repairing these roads and other facilities after the temple earned World Heritage status.

When Abhisit became prime minister, he vowed to protect the disputed area of 4.6 square kilometres around the temple, to have the World Heritage status cancelled, and to oppose Cambodia's attempt to develop the temple area as a World Heritage site. When PAD rallied in front of the UNESCO office in Bangkok in late July 2010 in order to pressure the WHC not to accept Cambodia's management plan for the temple, Abhisit expressed his appreciation toward PAD for showing concern for the country.[46]

In June 2009, a Thai delegation headed by Suwit Khunkitti, the minister of natural resources and environment, attended the WHC's 33rd session in Seville, Spain, with the objective of asking the WHC to review the temple's World Heritage status.[47] Cambodia was supposed to submit a Management Plan for WHC approval but had not completed the plan and thus requested to postpone the submission for a year. The request was agreed without any problem. However, the Abhisit government misinformed the Thai public that Suwit's team had won a temporary victory for Thailand by delaying the listing of the temple for a year, and vowed to continue this obstruction campaign at the 2010 WHC meeting. In fact, the temple had been listed since July 2008, yet all the Thai press, TV, and radio reported this piece of deliberate misinformation and credited the Abhisit government with effective lobbying to protect the national interest.[48] The Thai media were not only badly informed on such an important issue but were so blinded by nationalism that they failed to verify information and exercise good judgement and common sense. Later, only the *Bangkok Post* published a statement by Pongpol Adireksarn, head of the Thai World Heritage Committee, correcting the misinformation, while the Thai-language media did not bother to correct the mistake.[49]

The unrelenting opposition to the temple listing by the Abhisit government and PAD provoked an angry response from Hun Sen. The timing of his first strike was delicate. Just a few days before the start of an ASEAN Summit in October 2009 in Hua Hin, Thailand, Hun Sen disclosed to the media that he had offered Thaksin a position as his economic advisor, and that he would certainly not allow Thaksin to be extradited from Cambodia to serve his jail term in Thailand if the Thai government were to make a request. Abhisit retaliated by saying that "(ASEAN) has no time to pay attention to a person who wants to destroy ASEAN unity. And I hope Prime Minister Hun Sen will receive the right information and change his mind on the matter."[50] Hostility between Thailand and Cambodia overshadowed the ASEAN Summit chaired by Abhisit from the very first day.

When Thaksin arrived in Phnom Penh at the invitation of Hun Sen and Cambodia rejected Thailand's call for his extradition, relations sank to rock bottom. Bangkok immediately recalled its ambassador to Cambodia and Phnom Penh reciprocated. In addition, Abhisit announced that his government would cancel the Memorandum of Understanding, signed between the governments of Hun Sen and Thaksin in 2001, regarding maritime boundary demarcation and joint development of gas and oil reserves in the Gulf of Thailand. Abhisit justified the suspension on grounds that the MOU had been signed by Thaksin who had now become Cambodia's economic advisor and was in a position to leak confidential information to Cambodia. Abhisit's rationale was, however, misleading. Though the MOU was initiated during the Thaksin government, there had been little progress on either demarcation or joint development.[51] Several experts warned Abhisit that his overreaction to Hun Sen might jeopardize Thailand's long-term interests.[52] Abhisit further told the media that his government would consider suspending a soft loan for road construction in Cambodia.[53]

As described in chapter 2, Hun Sen reacted by rejecting all Thai assistance and challenging Abhisit to close the border. He accused Abhisit of meddling in Cambodia's internal affairs since the Thai government had not issued objections to other countries that had offered Thaksin an advisory position. He described Abhisit as an inexperienced politician who had stolen the premiership from the People's Power Party which had won an electoral majority, while Hun Sen himself was proud to be supported by two-thirds of the votes in the Cambodian parliament.[54]

After this spat, Abhisit's popularity rating shot up from 21.6 percent in October to 60 percent in November 2009, the highest surge since he took office in late 2008.[55] The PAD leaders urged him to revoke more bilateral agreements with Cambodia.[56] However, when the Cambodian government sent a letter asking to cancel the loan which Abhisit had threatened to suspend, Abhisit backtracked and told journalists that it was a misunderstanding on the part of Cambodia because his government had only floated the idea of a suspension and had not made a decision on the loan.[57] The same was also true for the

2001 MOU on the maritime boundary. While the Thai public was led to believe that the MOU had been revoked to protect national resources from Thaksin's exploitation, they were bewildered to hear in early November 2010 that Suthep Thueksuban, deputy prime minister and secretary-general of Democrat Party, had tried several times to seek a secret deal with Hun Sen over oil and gas development in the disputed maritime area, but had been snubbed by Hun Sen on grounds that the approach lacked transparency.[58] Abhisit and his party members could not provide clear answers about this leaked information which revealed that the announcement of the MOU suspension had been simply a political ploy to please Thai nationalists by showing that Thailand was still strong enough to punish an arrogant neighbour. The incident showed that the Democrat Party often preached about good governance and transparency, but acted otherwise.

Relations cooled for a while until the approach of the next annual WHC meeting in Brazil in July 2010. Suwit Khunkitti headed the Thai delegation, tasked to secure the removal of the temple from the World Heritage list and to block Cambodia's management plan for the temple area. Before the meeting took place, Abhisit threatened that Thailand would withdraw from WHC membership if the management plan were approved, and would not discuss the management plan until the border in the temple area was properly defined. Again, Suwit gave a false and confusing report of the WHC meeting to the Thai public. He told journalists that his lobbying had convinced the WHC to postpone discussion on Cambodia's management plan for the temple until its next meeting in Bahrain. He even added that the decision was taken partly because Cambodia failed to follow proper procedure in submitting the plan before the deadline of 10 February, but had made the submission less than 24 hours before the meeting and then decided to withdraw it.[59] He alleged that Cambodia had earmarked part of the disputed area for a development project, though in another report he admitted that he did not have an opportunity to see the plan at all. Suwit's team was applauded by the Thai media and the nationalists.[60]

The merriment soon subsided when Cambodia's Council of Ministers issued a rebuttal of Suwit's claims, stating that Cambodia had submitted its management plan and its report on the state of conservation of the temple to the World Heritage Centre, which acted as secretariat to the World Heritage

Committee, since January 2010, earlier than the 10 February deadline. The statement ridiculed the Thai government for not understanding WHC procedure since it was the duty of the WH Centre, not the WH Committee, to evaluate the management plan. The statement added that Cambodia had full authority to move forward on the basis of the management plan without authorization from the WHC as the site was under her sovereignty, but nonetheless welcomed recommendations and support from the transnational body. The statement went on to note that the WH Centre had actually evaluated the management plan and conservation report and had rendered an opinion that "it provides a good vision for the conservation of the World Heritage property as well as a solid basis on which the National Authority for the Protection of Preah Vihear can develop its policies and operational procedures". At the Brazil meeting, the WHC had then endorsed the report produced by the WH Centre.[61]

The incident was rather absurd and embarrassing for the Abhisit government. However, most mainstream Thai media chose to avoid the issue, possibly in an attempt to save face for Abhisit as well as for themselves. The government had been so bent on getting the temple delisted that it had apparently failed to do its homework, particularly over the working procedure of the WHC. Moreover, in February 2010, several months before the 2010 WHC meeting in Brazil, Cambodia's Office of the Council of Ministers had issued a statement denying Suwit's claim that the listing of the temple was incomplete because Cambodia had yet to file its site management plan. In this statement, Cambodia informed the Thai government that it had submitted the updated conservation report and the final management plan to the WHC since 28 January 2010, and that it had begun to develop the whole area of the temple with the collaboration of UNESCO and international experts.[62] If the Thai government had wanted to find out what development was under way in the temple vicinity, it could have obtained the information from the website of the Cambodian government.[63] The Thai media might have been nonplussed by such a confident assertion from Cambodia, but again failed to investigate the truth about this matter and continued to harbour hopes that Thailand had a chance to oppose Cambodia's management plan at the next WHC session in mid-2011.

Other Actors

Business sector

Whenever Thailand's relations with a neighbouring country become heated, villagers living near the border are affected by cross-border fighting, and cross-border trade and investment are disrupted. While villagers' voices command little attention from the government, business can have considerable influence on government's actions. This was clearly borne out on the Thai-Myanmar border. Whenever the Myanmar military junta was unhappy with Bangkok, it did not hesitate to close down the border without warning. Though the closure greatly affected consumers inside Myanmar, the junta was not concerned since Myanmar people did not dare to make a complaint against the totalitarian regime anyway. However, the junta knew that the Thai business sector would protest loudly at the losses they suffered, that the Thai media would run stories detailing losses of several hundred million baht of exports per day, and that the Thai government would react by trying to persuade the Myanmar regime to reopen the border as soon as possible. Though this pressure effectively reduced the bargaining power of the Thai government against its Myanmar counterpart on whatever issue was at hand, the Thai governments usually responded to the business sector's demand for action. The Myanmar regime understood this arrangement very well and had regularly used border closures to bluff the Thai government since the two countries re-established bilateral relations in the late 1980s.

When the spat with Cambodia deteriorated to the point that both sides recalled their ambassadors, there was widespread concern that the Abhisit government's next step would be to close the borders. But Abhisit quickly reassured the business sector that his government would try not to let the conflict affect border trade. Moreover, while on the front stage Abhisit was playing tough toward Cambodia, another cabinet member was on a low profile trip to promote economic cooperation with Cambodia. In September 2010, deputy commerce minister Alongkorn Ponlaboot led a group of Thai business people by road into Cambodia and Vietnam in order to explore economic opportunities. Alongkorn told the press that the Abhisit government wished to regain its status as the leading investor in

Cambodia, and had laid plans to establish a special economic zone at Ban Parai in Aranyaprathet District to promote ties with Cambodia. This zone would offer comprehensive import-export services including distribution centres, customer services, and an industrial estate. The zone would be linked with Cambodia's Poipet-O'Neang Special Economic Zone.[64]

Representatives of Thai business in Cambodia also made their concern known to the public.[65] Yet while business groups on the Myanmar-Thailand border usually made loud calls for immediate reopening of their border, Thai business in Cambodia made their plea in a much softer tone. At a public forum in Thammasat University, three Thai entrepreneurs talked about the hardship they endured when they first set up businesses in war-torn Cambodia in the early 1990s, and claimed they were now facing fierce competition from Vietnam. They urged the government not to do anything that would harm their businesses, and warned that their loss would mean Vietnam's gain with little or no negative consequences for Cambodian consumers. These Thai business people were probably sensitive to nationalist feelings among the Thai public. They also did not want to sound narrowly concerned with their own personal interest while neglected national interest as defined by the Yellow Shirt movement. Their plea was tuned to kindle sympathy from the audience and the media.[66]

The Military

During the early stages of the PAD campaign on the Preah Vihear temple, several military leaders including the army commander, supreme commander, and chief of staff came out to defend the Samak government's endorsement of Cambodia's proposal to list the temple as a World Heritage site as discussed in Chapter III. However, when the nationalist campaign heated to the point it might torch any opponents, these military figures made no further attempt to defend the Samak government or counterbalance the Yellow Shirts' misinformation. They concentrated on cooling down the border situation to prevent it flaring up into a war.

Diplomatic spats between leaders in the country capitals often lead to tension along the border. When the two countries recalled their ambassadors, the Thai military leaders tried to lessen tension at the border by such tactics as inviting the Cambodian minister of defence, General Tea Banh, to play golf in Thailand, and organizing a football match between Thai and Cambodian soldiers stationed around the Preah Vihear area.[67]

When the PAD's popularity declined during the Abhisit government, the military sometimes became openly critical. After a PAD group led by Vira Somkhwamkit tried to draw attention to the Preah Vinar issue by crossing the border into Cambodian territory and being arrested by the Cambodian authorities, the commander of the Second Region Army, Lieutenant General Thawatchai Samutsakorn, told journalists that tension along the border was created by people who never listened to others and tried to stir up conflict. He asked "all patriots not to create problems for the country".[68] When Thai and Cambodian troops exchanged fire in February 2011, the army commander General Prayuth Chan-ocha sarcastically summoned those eager to wage war with Cambodia to come to the border and fight.[69]

While military leaders were unhappy with the PAD, they never contradicted the PAD's propaganda linking the World Heritage listing with the potential loss of 4.6 square kilometres of disputed territory. They already had their hands full managing street politics in the capital and a bloody crisis in the three southernmost provinces. They had no wish to open up another front on the Cambodian border, particularly against ex-Khmer Rouge cadres, now part of the Cambodian army, who knew the area very well.

The military's obvious lack of enthusiasm for a war against Cambodia made them vulnerable to harassment by the Yellow Shirts who mocked the army as cowardly and shameful because they refused to respond to PAD's calls for them to strike at Cambodia. The PAD leader, Sondhi Limthongkul, urged the army to occupy Angkor Wat and then negotiate an exchange of Angkor Wat for the Preah Vihear temple and its surrounding area.[70] This barrage of propaganda seems to have provoked the army to prove its nationalist credentials. During border clashes in early February 2011, news reports in Thailand showed that firing by Thai troops firing had caused damage to the temple and inflicted a heavy toll on the Cambodian forces. The army spokesman proudly told the public that the incident proved that the Thai army was never afraid of Cambodia and was always ready to protect Thai territory![71]

With such incidents, the confrontation on the border became increasingly critical. In late March 2011, there were clashes at another part of the border in Surin province around two Angkorean-style stupas of Ta Muean Thom and Ta Khwai (or Ta Krabey in Khmer). Thailand and Cambodia both claimed sovereignty over these two sites. The clashes lasted for two weeks and resulted in a total of ten deaths. As always, both sides blamed each other for starting the firing. The Cambodian side claimed that the Thai military had started the firing in order to increase its leverage in domestic politics; the firing coincided with rumours of another coup and crackdown on opposition voices. The Thai side claimed that the Cambodian government hoped the border clashes would create the conditions for a third party, such as ASEAN or the UN Security Council, to intervene in the conflict because the Abhisit government had consistently rejected any third party involvement even when bilateral mechanisms were patently incapable of resolving the issue.

The point here is that the role and attitude of the Thai military has been shaped by domestic politics and Thai-Cambodian relations. Early in the conflict, the military tried to defuse the tension created by the PAD movement, but when nationalist feelings spread, particularly in response to Hun Sen's comments, the military felt it had to demonstrate its patriotism to the Thai public.

Foreign Ministry

Like the military leaders, high ranking officials at the Ministry of Foreign Affairs, who had worked to support Cambodia's listing of the temple, were quiet during the height of nationalist propaganda. Four senior officials, along with Samak and his cabinet members, became victims of nationalism when PAD took them to court on charges of causing Thailand to lose territory. The four were: Virasakdi Futrakul, permanent secretary of the Ministry of Foreign Affairs; Krit Kraijitti, director general of the Department of Treaties and Legal Affairs; Phitsanu Suwannachot, deputy director of the Department of East Asia; and ambassador Choedchu Raktabut.[72] Later, they were acquitted by the court. In a personal communication with the author, a senior Thai diplomat in Phnom Penh revealed his frustration with PAD as well as with Abhisit, whom he viewed as trying to please the nationalists.

Though Foreign Affairs officials kept silent in public, behind the scenes they sought means to counter the nationalist position on the temple issue through academic voices. In early 2010, a high-ranking official of the Department of Boundary Delimitation asked Professor Charnvit Kasetsiri to convene a group of academics to undertake a research project entitled "Our boundaries, our neighbours" with the objective of educating the Thai public about border disputes between Thailand and neighbouring countries, demonstrating how other countries had settled similar disputes in a peaceful manner, and encouraging the public to view neighbouring countries through the lens of economic and cultural relations rather than as enemies. Charnvit recruited a group of twelve other academics from various institutions, myself included, to investigate dispute settlement in Europe and Asia. The Ministry of Foreign Affairs also requested the team to produce a video presentation that would be easily understood by the average Thai. The output under seven titles[73] was published in a series of six books plus CD and DVD, distributed free to university libraries nationwide and to those who attended a series of seminars held in various regions of the country. When PAD heard of the project, Sondhi accused the Ministry of Foreign Affairs and this academic group of "khai chat" or treason.[74]

Nationalism Backfires

Around the time of the WHC meeting in Brazil in July 2010, when Cambodia's management plan for the temple was scheduled for approval, PAD started a new round of protest targeting the Abhisit government.

Abhisit was the darling of the anti-Thaksin movement, monarchists, and military leaders. With his upper middle class background, western education, and reputation as a Mr Clean, Abhisit was an ideal leader in the perception of the urban middle class. Even though he was surrounded by corruption-tainted politicians, that did not diminish his appeal. Compared to a military leader, he seemed to have more legitimacy and possibly more capability to head a government. The fall of the Samak and Somchai governments through the efforts of PAD paved the way for Abhisit to become prime minister.

Although the PAD's street protests undermined the legitimacy and strength of parliament, the Democrat Party refrained from any criticism of the PAD's illiberal ideology and violent methods. Some Democrat Party members spoke on PAD platforms. After the PAD had occupied Government House and the airports, the Abhisit government seemed reluctant to press criminal charges against the PAD leaders. PAD and the Democrats seemed to complement one another well.

Buoyed by their success in staging massive rallies against Thaksin, the PAD leaders decided to launch into electoral politics. In early June 2009, they set up a party titled "Kanmueang mai" or "New Politics", but maintained PAD as a vehicle for extra-parliamentary politics. To test the political waters, the New Politics Party put up candidates at elections for the Bangkok Metropolitan Council in August 2009. Although Bangkok had been the heartland of the Yellow Shirt movement, the New Politics Party failed to gain a single seat while the Democrat Party swept the majority. The defeat revealed that most of the anti-Thaksin public were still faithful Democrat voters. In other words, PAD and the Democrats were competing for virtually the same supporters. Now that the pro-Thaksin party had been dislodged from power, these people possibly saw no further use for the aggressive political tactics of PAD. In addition, the PAD leaders had fallen into disputes among themselves, involving vicious personal attacks and accusation of financial malpractice. When PAD launched a new campaign in mid-2010, it failed to draw the same level of mass support as before.

On the run-up to the WHC meeting in Brazil in July 2010, PAD and a splinter group called the Thai Patriots Network (TPN) held several rallies, demanding that the government remove Cambodians who had encroached on the disputed area, and revoke the MOU on the survey and demarcation of the land boundary which a Democrat-led government had signed in 2000. PAD pointed out that the 2000 MOU included the Annex 1 or Dongrek Map from the Mixed Commission which had caused Thailand to lose the Preah Vihear temple to Cambodia in the 1962 court battle. They argued that acceptance of the Annex 1 map in the MOU would result in

Thailand losing not only the 4.6 square kilometres adjacent to the temple, but also another 1.5 million rai (240,000 hectare) along the border in the provinces of Ubon Ratchathani, Sisaket, Surin, Sa Kaeo, Chanthaburi, and Trat, plus maritime areas with potential revenues from reserves of natural oil and gas.[75]

PAD presented no evidence in support of these exaggerated claims. In fact, considerable progress had been made on demarcating the Thai-Cambodian border. According to the Ministry of Foreign Affairs, 603 kilometres of the total 798 kilometres of land boundary had been demarcated by August 2010. Only 195 kilometres along the Dongrek range, including the location of the Preah Vihear temple, remained undefined.[76] The 2000 MOU had resulted in a peaceful resolution of a substantial part of this problematic border. As for the maritime boundary, the 2000 MOU and the Annex 1 map have nothing to do with this issue. The demarcation of the maritime boundary is the subject of a totally separate document, the *Memorandum of Understanding between the Royal Thai Government and the Royal Government of Cambodia regarding the area of their overlapping Maritime Claims of the Continental Shelf*, signed in Phnom Penh on 18 June 2001, and known as the 2001 maritime MOU.

Even so, the newly-formed Abhisit government seemed sensitive to the pressure from its former ally. Abhisit agreed to speak at a PAD rally and participate in a televised public debate with PAD representatives. Abhisit told the Yellow Shirt crowd that his government might revoke the 2000 MOU if it could not solve the border problem. He also promised PAD that he would never use the term "area of overlapping claims" for the 4.6 square kilometres on grounds that the land belonged to Thailand alone. Abhisit even agreed to a PAD demand that his government would use both diplomatic and military measures to deal with encroachment into the disputed area. This statement provoked a strong reaction from Phnom Penh, which accused Abhisit of threatening Cambodia's territorial sovereignty by force.[77]

When PAD continued to press for cancellation of the 2000 MOU, Abhisit retracted his promise to scrap it on grounds that the document was still useful. PAD also urged the government to withdraw from the WHC on the grounds if was biased in favour of Cambodia. Though prior to the WHC meeting in July 2010 Abhisit himself had threatened to withdraw from the WHC, he now refused to follow the PAD demand, saying that membership allowed Thailand to keep a watch on development of the temple.[78]

PAD continued to organize rallies on the territorial issue but failed to mobilize substantial mass support. While rallies against the pro-Thaksin governments had attracted tens of thousands, the new round of protests drew only a few hundred. PAD thus tried a new tactic. On 29 December 2011, seven people including a PAD leader Vira Somkhwamkit and a Democrat MP Panich Vikitsreth walked across the border into Cambodia and were arrested by Cambodian soldiers for illegal entry, trespassing on a military zone, and espionage. PAD leaders in Bangkok told journalists that the arrest had taken place on Thai territory and accused Cambodia of violating Thailand's sovereignty. However, the Abhisit government and Thai military leaders insisted that the group had indeed trespassed on Cambodian territory.[79] A video clip released anonymously on YouTube showed that the group had intentionally crossed the border and knew they were on Cambodian soil when they were arrested. Moreover, the clip revealed that Panich had informed Abhisit by phone about their plan of deliberate trespass.[80] The group perhaps believed that the Thai government would move quickly to secure their release because a Democrat MP was with them. The incident seems to have been designed to rekindle nationalist feeling against Cambodia and thus bring PAD back to the centrestage of Thai politics.

However, the Cambodian government refused to release the seven Thais and put them on trial. Five of them, including MP Panich, were sentenced to nine months in jail but soon set free and returned to Thailand after the court suspended their jail terms. But Vira and his secretary, Ratri Phiphathanaphaibun, were given harsher sentences of eight and six years in prison respectively, and Hun Sen refused to process a royal pardon for them.[81] PAD accused the Abhisit government of negligence over the case, and demanded the government act immediately to secure the release of this pair, use force to remove all Cambodians from the disputed area, and revoke the 2000 MOU. PAD gave the government a 4-day deadline to respond or else they would occupy Government House again with intent on bringing the government down.[82]

Beginning on 3 February 2011 and continuing for four days there were armed clashes in the disputed area near the temple. Eight people of both sides, including two Thai civilians, were killed, twenty soldiers were injured, and thousands of people living near the border had to flee their homes. Several houses in Phum Saron village in Sisaket Province were heavily damaged by artillery shells from the Cambodian side, while shelling from Thai troops caused some minor damage to the temple.[83] This was the most violent incident since the conflict over the temple started in 2008. Both sides accused each other of triggering the clash by encroaching on the 4.6 square kilometre disputed area. Cambodia said the Thai military was to blame for building a short road from the Kao Sikha Kiri Svara pagoda in the disputed area to Highway 221 on the Thai side. Cambodia demanded the Thais withdraw from this encroachment but the Thais countered by demanding Cambodia stop the construction of a road from Cambodian territory to the west of the temple.[84] In Bangkok, there were rumours that the border skirmishes were staged as a pretext for another coup to pre-empt a comeback by pro-Thaksin parties at a general election due by the end of 2011.

News of the bloody clashes buoyed PAD. At its rally site near Government House, PAD leaders praised the courage of the Thai military. Sondhi Limthongkul urged the government to "parade Thai troops" opposite Cambodia's Siem Reap and Battambang provinces, and employ gunboat diplomacy by sending naval craft to block Cambodia's sea lanes, in order to force Phnom Penh to negotiate with Thailand and put an end to the territorial conflict. Sondhi promised to send Yellow Shirt followers to the border area to boost Thai soldiers' morale.[85] When Abhisit rejected all the PAD demands, they condemned him as a dumb coward, liar, and corrupt leader. The rift between PAD and the Democrat party was now complete.[86] PAD accused the Abhisit government of being much worse than Thaksin in all aspects, including treason, corruption, and failure to solve economic problems.[87]

Abhisit condemned the skirmishes as part of a Cambodian strategy to internationalize a bilateral issue.[88] He pinned the blame for the renewed border tension on the WHC for listing the temple and considering the management plan. He demanded that the WHC refrain from considering the management plan until a solution to the border conflict was found.[89] He objected to the WHC sending a representative to investigate the damage to the temple. Though Abhisit's demands brought no formal response from the WHC, the clashes in practice halted, or at least delayed, any development around the temple area, as Thailand had wished. While Abhisit was opposed to the temple listing, he reiterated that Thailand wanted to settle the border dispute with Cambodia in a peaceful manner and within the existing bilateral mechanism without any mediation by a third party.

PAD was now committed to driving the Abhisit government out of office and, more importantly, paving the way for another military intervention or coup to prevent the forthcoming election. But PAD was increasingly isolated. Its month-long rally near Government House drew only a few hundred people, and the mainstream media criticized PAD as irrational troublemakers.

Suwit Khunkitti, the minister of natural resources and environment, led the Thai delegation to the WHC meeting in Paris on 25 June 2011. Shortly before, a general election had been announced for 3 July. Suwit was a candidate and leader of a minor party. At the Paris meeting, he suddenly announced that Thailand would withdraw from the WHC because the WHC had not met Thailand's request to postpone consideration of Cambodia's management plan for the temple. He explained to the press that this withdrawal would prevent Thailand from losing further territory. PAD leaders praised Suwit's action. But the WHC quickly issued a statement that it had held no discussion on the temple's management plan and that Suwit's claims were false. It seems Suwit had hoped to gain some nationalistic image for himself and his party at the election, but the attempt backfired and the party failed to win a single seat.[90]

Impasse, then Back to ICJ

Unlike Thailand, Cambodia was open to intervention by either ASEAN or the UN Security Council to help conciliate the dispute. Right after the February 2011 clash, Hun Sen announced that there would be no more bilateral talks as they patently failed to settle the territorial problem. Cambodia called on the UN Security Council to convene an urgent meeting to stop Thailand's aggression, and requested a UN peacekeeping force to contain violence in the disputed area. Thailand opposed any role for the UN.[91] The Council agreed to consider the issue but the session resulted in only a moderate statement urging both countries to display maximum restraint, establish a permanent ceasefire, and resolve the situation peacefully through dialogue with facilitation from Indonesia, the current ASEAN chair.[92] When Hun Sen proposed a permanent ceasefire, Abhisit immediately rejected the idea.[93]

Indonesia, represented by its foreign minister Marty Natalegawa, campaigned among the ASEAN members for the grouping to play a mediating role. Indonesia was ready to send a team of observers to the disputed area to monitor the ceasefire. Cambodia welcomed the proposal.[94] The Abhisit government initially agreed but then backtracked after Thai military leaders objected to any third party involvement, claiming it would undermine Thailand's sovereignty. The military claimed it had a patriotic duty to protect Thai territory, and the civilian leadership seemed unable to go against this stand. The military's power had significantly increased since the 2006 coup, discouraging any challenge from the civilian leadership.[95] Besides, the Abhisit government was widely believed to have been installed as a result of the army's power brokering, forcing other political parties to defect from the pro-Thaksin coalition. Yellow Shirt leaders also denounced any plan to allow an Indonesian team of observers into the area,[96] and Abhisit seemed reluctant to give the Yellow Shirts another opportunity to attack his government. Without agreement from Thailand, Indonesia could not send any team.

Frustrating by the deadlock, Cambodia submitted a request to the ICJ on 28 April 2011 to interpret the 1962 verdict on the location of the border in the disputed area. Cambodia could initiate this process unilaterally whether or not Thailand agreed. Cambodia also requested the Court to issue a provisional ruling that Thailand withdraw its troop from the disputed area, and refrain from action that interfered with Cambodia's right to develop the temple or that exacerbated the conflict.[97] While the case was under consideration by the ICJ, Abhisit requested a royal decree to dissolve parliament on 6 May 2011.

The Thai legal team argued that the ICJ had no jurisdiction over the case but the court brushed this aside and went ahead to issue several provisional rulings:[98]

1. Both countries must immediately withdraw their military personnel from a provisional demilitarized zone (PDZ) around the temple and refrain from any military presence within the PDZ and from any armed activity directed at the zone.
2. Thailand must not obstruct Cambodia's free access to the temple or Cambodia's provision of fresh supplies to its non-military personnel in the temple.
3. Thailand and Cambodia must continue their cooperation with ASEAN and must allow ASEAN-appointed observers into the PDZ.
4. Thailand and Cambodia must refrain from any action which might aggravate or extend the dispute or make it more difficult to resolve.

Kasit Piromya, now caretaker foreign minister, said these rulings were "fair to both parties", despite the fact that they restrained Thai actions in the disputed area.[99] Although the rulings required troops from both sides to withdraw, Hun Sen greeted the provisional measures as a slap in the face of Thailand and urged the Thai side to accept the decision. He reiterated his support for Indonesia playing a monitoring role.[100]

At the Thai election on 3 July, the Democrats suffered a defeat and Thaksin's sister, Yingluck Shinawatra, became prime minister. Hun Sen might have expected that the new government would implement the ICJ order to ensure peace at the border, but Yingluck had to deal with the military. In August 2011, the new defence minister General Yuthasak Sasiprapha told the press that Indonesian observers were not needed at all.[101] In November 2011, the Thai supreme commander General Thanasak Patiprakon stated that Thai troops would not withdraw from the disputed area and were not obliged to follow the instruction of the ICJ. The general said that withdrawing troops from the demilitarized zone would in practice mean ceding Thailand's sovereignty over the area: "If Thai troops have to seek approval from ASEAN observers before entering the disputed area, it means that the country has in practice lost its territory." He passed the buck to Yingluck by saying that the government had to issue a clear instruction if it wanted the armed forces to follow the ICJ instructions.[102] General Thanasak's reasoning was purely nationalistic. If Yingluck were to follow the ICJ order, she risked being branded as a weak leader who lacked the determination and courage to protect Thailand's national interest. Under such pressure, Yingluck complied, telling the press on the following day that her government would keep its troops in the disputed area and protect Thailand's national sovereignty along the border. Yingluck's cabinet bought some time by referring the matter to the Thai-Cambodian General Border Committee (GBC) and promising to convey the GBC's decision to parliament for approval.[103] This procedure would take several months or perhaps never reach completion.

The ICJ is expected to deliver its final decision around the end of 2013, but it is not certain that this will resolve the border dispute. If the decision were to assign the 4.6 square kilometres to Cambodia, it would cause a public uproar in Thailand, particularly if Thai politics were in a fragile state at the time, and result in another round of border tensions. Academics associated with PAD have already told the public that the Thai government would not have to comply with the ICJ order. The anti-Thaksin factions in the military and the civil society movement would seize on such an opportunity to advance their political position.

Summary

PAD's success in manipulating nationalist discourse against the pro-Thaksin governments depended crucially on support from various state and non-state bodies. People and institutions from varying backgrounds were united in a desire to root out the power of Thaksin and his proxies. The National Human Rights Commission, courts, senators, and media became involved. Although they were supposed to function as checks and balances, they were prepared to support PAD's anti-Thaksin campaign no matter how undemocratic, ultra-nationalistic, and uncivil PAD could be. As a result, they sacrificed their own credibility and people's trust. More astonishingly, they appeared to care very little about the impact on Thailand's relationship with Cambodia. Seemingly, this relationship could be sacrificed for domestic political gain.

While PAD supplied the leadership for the campaign, these supporting bodies provided moral and legal legitimacy. Against a background of political polarization, the nationalistic discourse on "lost territories" proved effective in discouraging criticism of PAD's arguments. The PAD campaign on the Preah Vihear temple was simply the means to achieve the end of rooting out Thaksin's power and strengthening the royalist-conservative domination of politics. Because the temple issue was just a tool, PAD could issue any demands, however outrageous and unrealistic. When governments failed to meet these unrealistic demands, PAD attacked them as unpatriotic, treasonous, weak, and ineffective. The PAD leaders probably had little real concern about the temple and the tiny piece of land beside it. Their demands, methods, and misinformation only complicated the issue and intensified the conflict with Cambodia, rather than leading to a solution. PAD's uncivil actions seemed to have been designed to sow misinformation, fan nationalist fire, and cultivate a sense of superiority and hatred toward Cambodia. These actions ran against the efforts of state agencies that are committed to promoting good neighbourly relations with Cambodia and overcoming historical antagonism (see Chapter II). Many state agencies disagreed with PAD's actions and were very careful not to aggravate the situation, but found it difficult to publicly criticize PAD given the atmosphere suffused with nationalistic emotions.

PAD's nationalist campaign resulted in the Thai public having a flawed perception of the temple issue, and prevented the two countries addressing the territorial dispute in a peaceful manner. Because Abhisit and the Democrat Party went along with PAD's nationalist campaign, when they found themselves in government they were hamstrung by this past. Abhisit had to play a delicate game, continuing to take a nationalistic stance over the temple and the border issue while simultaneously trying to insulate other aspects of cooperation with Cambodia against the nationalist fire. The Democrat-led government had more room to manoeuvre than its pro-Thaksin predecessors but its opposition to the listing of the temple as a World Heritage site precluded any chance that it would achieve any resolution of this historical problem.

Notes

1. Charnvit Kasetsiri, *Siamese/Thai nationalism and Cambodia*; Thongchai Winichakul, "Preah Vihear could be a Time Bomb", *The Nation*, 30 June 2008; Pavin Chachawalpongpun, "Embedding Embittered History: Unending Conflicts

in Thai-Cambodian Relations", *Asian Affairs* XLII, no. 1 (March 2012), pp. 81–102.

2. Kittirianglap and Hewison, "Social Movements and Political Opposition in Contemporary Thailand", pp. 454–60; Pye and Schaffar, "The 2006 Anti-Thaksin Movement in Thailand: An Analysis", pp. 39–44.

3. Kittirianglap and Hewison, "Social Movements and Political Opposition in Contemporary Thailand", p. 468.

4. Thongchai Winichakul, "Toppling Democracy", *Journal of Contemporary Asia* 38, no. 1 (February 2008), pp. 11–37.

5. Michael K. Connors and Kevin Hewison, "Introduction: Thailand and the 'Good Coup'", *Journal of Contemporary Asia* 38, no. 1 (February 2008), pp. 2–3.

6. Andrew Walker, "Phra Viharn: The Dividing Line in Thailand", *New Mandala*, (25 August 2008) <http://asiapacific.anu.edu.au/newmandala/2008/08/25/phra-viharn-the-dividing-line-in-thailand/> (accessed 5 December 2010); Pavin Chachavalpongpun, "Diplomacy under Siege: Thailand's Political Crisis and the Impact on Foreign Policy", in *Contemporary Southeast Asia* 31, no. 3 (December 2009), p. 461.

7. The L7017 series of maps was produced in 1971, and a year later, the Thai Royal Survey Department (TRSD) produced the L7018 series which provides more detail than the L7017 ones. The L7017 and L7018 series are available on the TRSD website.

   Both the L7017 and L7018 maps are based on a scale of 1:50,000 while the Annex I Map is 1:200,000. Therefore, the Thais claim that the L7017/7018 maps are more accurate than the Annex I Map. The PAD leaders and academics insisted on the authenticity and legality of these two maps, but they are used unilaterally by Thailand and have no legal binding force in any bilateral or multilateral treaties between Thailand and neighbouring countries. The Annex I map, which is part of a series of maps produced by the Franco-Siamese Boundary Commission, is recognized in the MOU 2000 between Thailand and Cambodia as part of documents for border delimitation.

   In addition, during the 1959–62 court hearing, the Thai legal team submitted to the court a map produced in 1935 by the TRSD, not the one produced (later) by the American survey team.

   See MFA, Thailand, *The Inscription of the temple of Preah Vihear*, p. 46; MFA, Thailand, *Khomun thi khonthai khuan sap kieo kap prasat phra wihan lae kan cheracha khet daen thai-kampucha* [Information on the Preah Vihear temple and the border negotiation between Thailand and Cambodia that Thai people should know] (Bangkok: 2008), p. 41 <http://www.rtsd.mi.th/MapInformationServiceSystem/index.php?option=com_content&view=article&id=8&Itemid=10>.

8. For examples, Srisak Vallibhodom, *Khaophrawihan raboetwela ananikhom* [The Preah Vihear temple: A time-bomb from colonialism] (Bangkok: Matichon

Publication, 2008); The Manager Editorial Board, *Prasat phrawihan khwamching thi khonthai tongru* [The Preah Vihear temple: The truth Thai people must know] (Bangkok: Baan Phra Athit Publication, 2008); Duangthida Rames, *Prasat phrawihan kap buengna buenglang praden khatyaeng thai-kampucha* [The Preah Vihear temple and the making of the Thai-Cambodian conflict] (Bangkok: Katha, n.d.); Suwit Theerasatwat, *Bueangluek kansiadindaeng lae panha prasat phrawihan chak ro so. 112 tueng patchuban* [Insight to the territory losses and the problem of the Preah Vihear temple from 1893 to the present] (Bangkok: the History Association, 2010).

9. Thongchai Winichakul, *Siam Mapped*; Thongchai Winichakul, "Prawattisatthai baep rachachatniyom: chak yukananikhom amphrang su rachachatniyom mai rue latthi sadet pho khong kradumphi thai nai patchuban" [The Thai royal nationalist history: From the era of crypto-colonialism to the new royal nationalism, or the contemporary Rama V Cult of the Thai bourgeoisie], *Sinlapa Watthanatham* 23, no. 1 (November 2001), pp. 55–65.

10. Charnvit Kasetsiri, *Siamese/Thai Nationalism and Cambodia*, pp. 34–77.

11. Adun chaesam khetkanchon phrawihan siang ruk dindaeng thai" [Adul exposes the Preah Vihear temple's buffer zone risks violating Thai territory], *ASTV Manager Online*, 18 July 2008 <www.manager.co.th/Politics/ViewNews. aspx?NewsID=9510000084451> (accessed 20 July 2008).

12. "Sewana prasat phrawihan kangkha mikhon yubueanglang yuyaeng" [Seminar on the temple of Preah Vihear, doubt somebody is behind the scene to incite problem], *Matichon*, 30 June 2008.

13. "Mong anakot khaophrawihan...thai tongruthan maisiakha ngo" [Gazing at the future of the Preah Vihear temple...Thais must not be fooled], *ASTV Manager Online*, 4 July 2008 <http://www.manager.co.th/Travel/ViewNews. aspx?NewsID=9510000082791> (accessed 30 July 2008).

14. "Pha konkong khmen hup khaophrawihan" [Exposing Cambodia's cheating to take over the Preah Vihear temple], *ASTV Manager Online*, 30 September 2009 <www.manager.co.th/QOL/ViewNews.aspx?NewsID=9520000114481> (accessed 14 January 2011).

15. "Sap thalaengkan ruam thai-khmen wiparit chae phonprayot thapson maeo-hun sen uea" [Trashing the vicious Thai-Cambodian Joint Communiqué, Uncovering Thaksin's and Hun Sen's enormous conflict of interests], *ASTV Manager Online*, 1 July 2008 <www.manager.co.th/Politics/ViewNews.aspx?NewsID=95100000 77227> (accessed 29 July 2008).

16. "PM, all seven ministers survive censure debate", *Bangkok Post*, 27 June 2008.

17. "Verdicts hammer govt", *Bangkok Post*, 9 July 2008; "Samak jibes at temple injunction", *Bangkok Post*, 7 August 2008.

18. "Samphat tej bunnag ratthamontri samsipkao wan" [Interview Tej Bunnag a 39-day Minister], *Matichon*, 15 September 2008.

19. "Samphan luek phonprayot longtua prasat phrawihan-thaksin-al fayet-po.to. tho." [Deep relation, a settlement of profit sharing on the Phreah Vihear Temple, Thaksin-Al Fayed-PTT], *ASTV Manager Online*, 22 July 2008 <http://www.manager.co.th/Daily/ViewNews.aspx?NewsID=9510000085750> (accessed 30 October 2008).

20. "Sap thalaengkan ruam thai-khmen wiparit chae phonprayot thapson maeo-hun sen uea" [Trashing the vicious Thai-Cambodian Joint Communiqué, Uncovering Thaksin's and Hun Sen's enormous conflict of interests], *ASTV Manager Online*, 1 July 2008 <www.manager.co.th/Politics/ViewNews.aspx?NewsID=951000007 7227> (accessed 29 July 2008); Wanwipa Charoonroj, "Yokluek m.o.u. 2544 phro lamoet phantha korani rairaeng" [Revoking the MOU 2001 for it violates the commitment severely] <www.praviharn.net/index.php?option=com_content& view=article&id=130:-mou-2544-new&catid=35:2009-08-01-23-00&itemid+148> (accessed 4 July 2010); "Surapong jayanama lok khrap kaeng phontok kimulai" [Surapong Jayanama expose the cockeyed gang], *ASTV Manager Online*, 31 October 2009 <www.thaiday.com/Daily/ViewNews.aspx?NewsID=952000 0130300> (accessed 30 October 2010).

21. "Hun sen ngam na hai sampathan namman khet thapson ao thai" [The shameless Hun Sen grants oil concession in the overlapping claimed area off the Gulf of Thailand], *ASTV Manager Online*, 23 July 2009 <www.manager.co.th/IndoChina/ViewNews.aspx?NewsID=9520000083341> (accessed 1 December 2010).

22. PTT Exploration and Production Public Com Ltd., "PTTEP Participation in Petroleum Block B, Cambodia, April 4, 2005" <http://www.pttep.com/en/newsDetail.aspx?ContentID=45> (accessed 28 February 2011).

23. Lim Vatha, "Petroleum Company and Management Project, Cambodia Case Study Update on Petroleum Activities in Cambodia", 21 February 2006 <http://www.ccop.or.th/ppm/document/CAWS6/CAWS6DOC04_vatha.pdf> (accessed 30 August 2008).

24. Despite a lack of substantial proof, in February 2012, the former finance minister of Abhisit's government still used such allegations to question whether the government of Yingluck Shinawatra was trying to facilitate Thaksin's business. "No plan to sell PTT: Kittirat", *The Nation*, 10 February 2012.

25. "Ko kong sunklang ratthaksin thalom thai" [Koh Kong, center of the Thaksin state to attack Thailand] *Kom chad luek*, 13 November 2009.

26. "Kantopto kamphucha: miti thangkotmai lae kantangprathet" [Response to Cambodia: the legal and foreign policy aspects], Paper for a public seminar forum organized by Faculty of Law, Chulalongkorn University on 16 November 2009.

27. "Phakonkong khmen hup khaophrawihan" [Exposing Cambodia's cheating to take over the Preah Vihear temple], *ASTV Manager Online*, 30 September 2009 <www.manager.co.th/QOL/ViewNews.aspx?NewsID=9520000114481> (accessed 14 January 2011).

28. Charnvit Kasetsiri was a founder of the undergraduate program on Southeast Asian Studies at Thammasat University — the first of its kind in Thailand.

29. They are Charnvit Kasetsiri, *Siam/Thai nationalism and Cambodia*; Puangthong Pawakapan, *Songkhram kankha lae chatniyom nai khwam samphan thai-kampucha* [Wars, Trade and Nationalism in Thai-Cambodian Relations] (Bangkok: The Foundation of the Textbooks Project, 2009); Thamrongsak Petchlert-anan, *Sayam thai kap dindaen nai kamphucha lae lao* [Siam-Thailand and "Territories" in Cambodia and Laos] (Bangkok: The Foundation of the Textbooks Project, 2009).

30. "Klangchat rue rakchat? Botrian chak prasatphrawihan" [Chauvinism or Patriotism? A lesson from the Preah Vihear temple], *Krungthep Turakij*, 7 March 2011; "Sap thalaengkan ruam thai-khmen wiparit chae phonprayot thapson maeo-hun sen uea" [Trashing the vicious Thai-Cambodian Joint Communiqué, uncovering Thaksin's and Hun Sen's enormous conflict of interests], *ASTV Manager Online*, 1 July 2008 <www.manager.co.th/Politics/ViewNews.aspx?NewsID=9510000077227> (accessed 29 July 2008); Surawit Wirawan, "Prathet khong khon thai chai khmen" [The Nation of Thais with Khmer Hearts], *Manager Online*, 13 January 2011 <http://www.manager.co.th/Daily/ViewNews.aspx?NewsID=9540000004737> (accessed 14 January 2011).

31. "Klangchat rue rakchat? Botrian chak prasat phrawihan" [Chauvinism or Patriotism? A lesson from the Preah Vihear temple], *Krungthep Turakij*, 7 March 2011.

32. For example, see the first question of the interview in "Akkarapong khamkhoon chaeng huachai mai chai khmen" [Akkarapong Khamkhoon cries my heart is not Khmer], *Krungthep Turakij*, 3 March 2011.

33. Michael Hayes, "The View from Cambodia", *Phnom Penh Post*, 17 February 2011.

34. Apart from Sondhi Limthongkul's *Manager* media group, major newspapers such as *Khom Chad Luek, Thai Post, The Nation, Post Today, Daily News, Naew Na, and Krungthep Turakij* ran concerted nationalist attacks on Cambodia.

35. "Editorial", *Khom Chad Luek*, 13 November 2009.

36. "Thaksin-hun sen songkhram namlai thi thuk pokpit, khmen…prathet mi wai khai" [Thaksin-Hun Sen, the disguised war of words, Cambodia…a country for sale?], *Khom Chad Luek*, 11 November 2009. Examples of daily headlines and article titles show how the mainstream Thai media portrayed the temple issue, such as, "Hun sen-thaksin yam thai khao khmen tiw kunsue" [Hun Sen-

Thaksin insult Thailand! Enter Cambodia to coach the mastermind], *Khom Chud Luek*, 9 November 2009; Sunan Srichantra, "Ta to ta fun to fun phue daikhuen khaophrawihan" [An eye for an eye, a tooth for a tooth for the return of the Preah Vihear temple], *Nation Weekly*, 5 October 2009.

37. "Mo. tho. sho nganwichai 24 withi thi ratthaban thaksin saeksaeng sue" [TU's research reveals Thaksin's 24 methods of interfering with media], *Prachatai*, 24 November 2008 <http://www.prachatai.com/journal/2008/11/18937> (accessed 24 November 2008).

38. The National Human Rights Commission of Thailand, "Open letter from the NHRC, Thailand to Ban Ki-Moon, dated July 28, 2008", *Prachatai*, 29 July 2008 <www.prachatai.com/english/node/716> (accessed 28 July 2008).

39. "Samphap phiset saneh chammarik" [Special interview with Saneh Chammarik], *Prachatai*, 26 December 2006 <http://prachatai3.info/m/journal/11064> (accessed 26 December 2006).

40. "Court orders revocation of Preah Vihear joint communiqué", *Bangkok Post*, 29 December 2008.

41. "Verdicts hammer govt", *Bangkok Post*, 9 July 2008.

42. "Worajet yan lakwicha sanpokkhrong maimi khetamnatsan nuea khadi khaophrawihan" [Worajet insists the Administrative Court has no jurisdiction over the Preah Vihear temple case], *Prachatai*, 1 July 2008 <http://prachatai. com/journal/2008/07/17229> (accessed 2 July 2008).

43. Chamnan Chanrueng, "Kanchai amnattulakan an pen issara kap kankrathamphit to tamnaengnathi nai kanyutthitham" [The exercise of independent judicial power and the abuse of judicial power], *Prachatai*, 9 March 2001 <http:// prachatai.com/journal/2011/03/33456> (accessed 9 March 2001).

44. "Worajet Phakeerat: san khian rattathammanun mai" [Worajet Pakeerat: Court writes a new constitution], *Prachatai*, 17 July 2008 <http://prachatai.com/ journal/2008/07/17353> (accessed 17 July 2008).

45. See full text of Abhisit's parliamentary debate on June 24, 2008 <www.praviharn. net/images/stories/apisit_word_to_word.pdf> (accessed 1 October 2010).

46. "PM thanks rally, blames Noppadon", *Bangkok Post*, 1 August 2010.

47. "Govt renew Preah Vihear push", *Bangkok Post*, 18 June 2009.

48. For example, "Khammakan moradok lok luean phicharana khuen thabian phrawihan pina" [The World Heritage Committee postpones the inscription of the Phreah Vihear temple to next year], *Matichon*, 30 June 2009; Mass Communication of Thailand (MCOT), English News, "Thai PM says delayed Preah Vihear temple World Heritage Site registration could solve problems", 30 June 2009 <www.southeastasianarchaeology.com/2009/07/01/thailand-hopes-for-a-delay-in-preah-vihear-registration> (accessed 1 February 2011).

49. "Pongpol: temple's listing irreversible", *Bangkok Post*, 1 July 2009.

50. "Hun Sen, Abhisit start summit war of words", *Bangkok Post*, 24 October 2009.

51. "Mark ngat sonthisanya la no. cho. maeo leng yokradap to khmen hak duephang" [Mark (Abhisit) employs treaty to hunt for the convicted Thaksin, aims to toughen measure against Cambodia if recalcitrant], *ASTV Manager Online*, 10 September 2009 <http://www.manager.co.th/Politics/ViewNews. aspx?NewsID=9520000135334> (accessed 10 September 2009).

52. For example, "Navy chief warns govt on MOU", *Bangkok Post*, 21 November 2009; "Editorial", *Matichon*, 14 November 2009; "Nakwichakan ting luek m.o.u. thai sia- lai chat chong suamprayot nai khamen" [Academics warns Thailand would lose if MOU invoked — many countries wait to take over advantages in Cambodia], *Krunthep Turkij*, 22 November 2009.

53. "Cabinet revokes MOU on maritime border", *Bangkok Post*, 11 November 2009.

54. "Hun Sen blames Thailand (and Abhisit) all the way", *Bangkok Post*, 12 November 2010.

55. "Abhisit's govt needs to redefine the national interest", *Bangkok Post*, 13 November 2009.

56. "Cancel other pacts, financial aid projects to Cambodia, PAD urges", *Bangkok Post*, 8 November 2009.

57. "Cambodia B1.4bn loan still on", *Bangkok Post*, 29 November 2009; "Road funds for Cambodia unfrozen", *Bangkok Post*, 28 August 2010.

58. "Prakat luanglok chak bantuek m.o.u. 2544 tueng moradoklok" [The deceptive announcement, from the 2001 MOU to the world heritage], *Matichon*, 5 September 2011 <http://www.matichon.co.th/news_detail.php?newsid=1315192414&grp id=01&catid&subcatid> (accessed 5 September 2011).

59. "WHC postpones decision on temple plan to next year", *Bangkok Post*, 30 July 2010; "Errors stall Cambodian temple bid", *Bangkok Post*, 31 July 2010.

60. "Bueangluek patibatkan hak khamen lom phaenchatkan phrawihan" [Insight into an operation to topple Cambodia's management plan for the temple of Preah Vihear], *Matichon*, 31 July 2010 <http://www.matichon.co.th/play_clip. php?newsid=1280528257> (accessed 31 July 2010).

61. See Office of Council of Ministers, Cambodia, "Summary of the Results of the 34th Session of the World Heritage Committee", 2 August 2010 <//ki-media. blogspot.com/2010/08/summary-of-results-of-34th-session-of.html> (accessed 30 August 2010); The National Committee for the World Heritage, "Statement dated September 3, 2010" <www.pressocm.gov.kh/PRESS-RELEASE/PR2010/ ST03092010_EN_01.pdf> (accessed 13 January 2011).

62. Office of Council of Ministers, Cambodia, "Clarification No. 007/PRU/2010

dated February 12, 2010" <www.pressocm.gov.kh/PRESS-RELEASE/PR2010/CLA_11022010_ENG.pdf> (accessed 13 January 2010).

63. See the progress and management reports on <www.khmergovernmentoffice.org/publishing/PUB2010/PUB_05082010_ENG.pdf>.

64. "Diplomacy set to pay dividend in Cambodia", *Bangkok Post*, 6 September 2010.

65. "Kankha trat phang lang thai riak thut klap chak khmen" [The border trade at Trad suffers after Thailand recalls the ambassador], *Matichon*, 5 November 2009; "Thai-kamphucha rop krathop kankha turakit thong thieo don naksut wan song sinkha wietnam sadut" [Thai-Cambodia battle will affect trade, tourism will be hardest hit, fear export to Vietnam affected], *Matichon*, 9 February 2011.

66. "Sewana hua ok khon thai lae thurakit thai nai kamphucha" [Seminar on the faith of Thai people and business in Cambodia], *Prachatai*, 12 November 2009 <www.prachatai.com/journal/2009/11/26555> (accessed 13 November 2009).

67. "Tea Banh tueng thai ti golf prawit" [Tea Banh arrives Thailand to play golf with Prawit], *Khom Chud Luek*, 26 November 2009.

68. "Mo. tho. pho. 2 at khon bang klum mi khwam kit yai sang panha mai ru chop" [The Second Regional Army chief slams the politically ambitious group, creating never ending problems], *Matichon*, 31 December 2010.

69. "Pho. bo. tho. bo. lan khrai yak rop choen ma thi phra wihan"[Army Chief says anyone want to fight, please come to the Preah Vihear temple], *Matichon*, 4 February 2011.

70. "Sondhi lai prayut pai len li-ke pen thahan mai pokpong phaendin" [Sondhi tells Prayuth to be a folk dancer if he does not want to protect the land], *ASTV Manager Online*, 5 February 2011 <www.manager.co.th/Politics/ViewNews.aspx?NewsID=9540000015954> (accessed 5 February 2011; "Sondhi yu khop thap buk yuet nakhon wat laek prasat phra wihan" [Sondhi urges army to occupy Angkor Wat in exchange for the return of the Preah Vihear temple], *Prachatai*, 8 February 2011 <http://prachatai.com/journal/2011/02/33005> (accessed 8 February 2011).

71. "Wethi panthamit prop mue hai thahan thai lang patha khmen" [PAD's rally applauds Thai soldiers after clash with Cambodia], *Prachatai*, 4 February 2011 <http://prachatai.com/journal/2011/02/32959> (accessed 4 February 2011).

72. "Che pong hoem pak sia prachot chuan phanthamit klap ban noi chai khao phra thep borichak kha thanai 4 kha ratchakan thuek phanthamit fong", [Anchalee bad mouthing, upset news of Princess Sirindhon donates money to help four bureaucrats accused by the PAD], *Thai Insider*, 3 October 2008 <//thaienews.blogspot.com/2008/10/4_6567.html> (accessed 10 October 2008).

73. They are Pichet Saiphan and Suriya Khamwaan, *Khetdaen viatnam-chin-*

kamphucha-lao [Boundaries of Vietnam-China-Cambodia-Laos] (Bangkok: The Social Science and Humanity Textbooks Project, 201); Puangthong Pawakapan and Ronnaphol Masantisuk, *Khetdaenchin-rutsia-mongkolia* [Boundaries of China-Russia and Mongolia] (Bangkok: The Social Science and Humanity Textbooks Project, 2011); Morakot Jaewjinca Meyer and Akkarapong Khamkhoon, *Khetdaen farangset-nethoeland-maenam danub* [Boundaries of France-The Netherlands and the Danube River] (Bangkok: The Social Science and Humanity Textbooks Project, 2011); Onanong Thippimon, Thanasak Saichampa, Dulayaphak Preecharat, Supalak Kanchanakhundee, and Akkarapong Khamkhoon, *Khetdaen sayam/thai-malesia-phama-lao-kamphucha* [Boundaries of Siam/Thailand-Malaysia-Burma-Laos-Cambodia] (Bangkok: The Social Science and Humanity Textbooks Project, 2011); Charnvit Kasetsiri, *Collected Treaties-Conventions-Agreements-Memorandum of Understanding and Maps, Between Siam/Thailand-Cambodia-Laos-Burma-Malaysia* (Bangkok: The Social Science and Humanity Textbooks Project, 2011); Panat Tassaneeyanont, Prasit Piwawatthanapanich, and Wiphol Kitithasanasonchai, *Sanlok-sananuyatotulakan kapkhophiphatrawangprathet* [International Court of Justice-Permanent Court of Arbitration] (Bangkok: The Social Science and Humanity Textbooks Project, 2011). The 90-minute documentary film "Our Boundaries, Our Neighbors", can be viewed on the Textbook Project's website <http://textbooksproject.org/?page_id=821> as well as on YouTube at <http://www.youtube.com/watch?v=W7gqf3WwcwM>.

74. "Sondhi chuak nak wichakan appayot mark nak prachatippatai chom plom" [Sondhi attacks disgraceful academics — Abhisit the fake Democrat], *Manager Online*, 10 February 2011 <www.manager.co.th/asp-bin/mgrview.aspx?NewsI D=9540000017891> (accessed 10 February 2011).

75. "PM rejects land loss claims", *Bangkok Post*, 5 July 2010; "Chicha ta thai sia dindaen? Chuad sappayakon mahasan hak unesco rap phaen khmen" [Thai will lose enormous natural resources if UNESCO accepts Cambodia's plan], *Thairath*, 29 July 2010; "Kham to kham sondhi chi loek m.o.u. 43 kon sia 1.5 lan rai hai khmen" [Work by word, Sondhi urges to revoke MOU 2000 before losing 1.5 million rai to Cambodia], *ASTV Manager Online*, 24 July 2553 <http://www.manager.co.th/politics/ViewNews.aspx?NewsID=9530000102053> (accessed on 4 December 2010).

76. See Puangthong Pawakapan, "Prasat khao phra wihan, m.o.u. 2543, lae phaenthi" [The Preah Vihear temple, MOU 2000, and map], *Matichon*, 3 August 2010.

77. "Govt and PAD arm reach temple accord", *Bangkok Post*, 9 August 2010; "Abhisit and PAD at loggerheads over the temple issue", *Bangkok Post*, 8 August 2010.

78. "Po. cho. po. khan phanthamit sanoe thon tua chak phaki moradok lok" [Democrat opposes PAD's call to withdraw from the World Heritage Committee], *ASTV Manager Online*, 4 December 2010 <www.manager.co.th/Politics/ViewNews. aspx?NewsID=9530000171204> (accessed 20 December 2010).

79. "Arrested Thais were on Cambodian territory: Kasit", *The Nation*, 1 January 2011.

80. "Thailand Democrat MP and PAD Yellow Shirt invade Cambodia territory#2", <www.youtube.com/watch?v=RwwDhuv-RX0> (accessed 10 January 2011).

81. "Hun Sen rules out helping with pardon", *Bangkok Post*, 18 February 2011.

82. "Had PAD lost its conscience?", *Bangkok Post*, 9 February 2011.

83. "Govt spurns help from the UN", *Bangkok Post*, 9 February 2011.

84. "Thai and Cambodia troop clash for fourth day on border", 7 February 2011 <http://www.reuters.com/article/2011/02/07/us-thailand-cambodia-idUSTRE7151K320110207> (accessed 10 April 2012).

85. "Wethi panthamit prop mue hai thahan thai lang patha khmen" [PAD's rally applauds Thai soldiers after clash with Cambodia], *Prachatai*, 4 February 2011 <http://prachatai.com/journal/2011/02/32959> (accessed 4 February 2011); "Had PAD lost its conscience?", *Bangkok Post*, 9 February 2011.

86. "Sondhi at mark ya tuang thanon 2 len lai hai pai thuang 4.6 to. ro. ko. mo." [Sondhi attacks Abhisit, don't reclaim the 2 lane road, go reclaim the 4.6 sq. km.], *Prachatai*, 11 February 2011 <http://prachatai.com/journal/2011/02/33065> (accessed 11 February 2011).

87. "Phanthamit chi abhisit leo kwa thaksin 3 thao" [PAD says Abhisit is three times worse than Thaksin], *Prachatai*, 10 March 2011 <http://prachatai.com/journal/2011/03/33468> (accessed 10 March 2011).

88. Reuters, "Thai and Cambodia troops clash for fourth day on border", 7 February 2011 <www.reuters.com/article/2011/02/07/us-thailand-cambodia-idUSTRE7151K320110207> (accessed on 10 April 2012).

89. "PM urges Unesco to end chaos", *Bangkok Post*, 11 February 2011.

90. "UNESCO Director-General regrets the announcement of Thailand's intention to denounce the 1972 World Heritage Convention" 26 June 2011 <http://whc.unesco.org/en/news/772> (accessed 28 June 2011).

91. "Diplomacy the new Battlefront", *The Nation*, 8 February 2011.

92. International Crisis Group, *Waging Peace: ASEAN and the Thai-Cambodian Border Conflict*, Asia Report No. 215, 6 December 2011, p. 20.

93. "Abhisit rejects Hun Sen's ceasefire plan", *Bangkok Post*, 18 February 2011.

94. "ASEAN mission welcome to monitor Thai-Cambodian border, Kasit says", *The Nation*, 24 February 2011.

95. International Crisis Group, *Waging Peace*, pp. 21–23.

96. "Ruk poet wethi khao phra wihan tan sanlok tan thon thahan ham Indonesia chun" [Move to open the Preah Vihear temple forum, oppose World Court, oppose troop withdrawal, bar Indonesia's interference], *ASTV Manager Online*, 4 March 2012 <http://www.manager.co.th/South/ViewNews.aspx?NewsID=9550000028766> (accessed 10 April 2012).

97. "Cambodia files an Application requesting interpretation of the Judgment

rendered by the Court on 15 June 1962 in the case concerning the temple of Preah Vihear (Cambodia v. Thailand) and also asks for the urgent Indication of Provisional Measures", press release, ICJ, 2 May 2011.

98. "Request for interpretation of the judgment of 15 June 1962 in the case concerning the temple of Preah Vihear (Cambodia v. Thailand) and Request for the Indication of Provisional Measures", Order, ICJ, 18 July 2011.

99. Daniel Ten Kate and Anuchit Nguyen, "Thailand to Comply with Cambodian temple DMZ Imposed by UN", *Bloomberg*, 18 July 2011 <http://www.bloomberg.com/news/2011-07-18/thailand-to-comply-with-cambodian-temple-dmz-imposed-by-un.html> (accessed 10 April 2012).

100. "Cambodian PM Hun Sen: Thailand must honour the Court decision; Indonesian observers are a must", *Nokorwat News Daily*, 27 July 2011 <http://nokorwatnews.com/detailnews.php?newsid=12920&mnu=2&cid=4> (accessed 10 April 2012).

101. "Thailand says Indonesian observers not needed in disputed Cambodia border area", *Bangkok Post*, 20 August 2011.

102. "Thai troops stay put in the temple area", *Bangkok Post*, 23 November 2011.

103. "Troops to remain near Preah Vihear", *Bangkok Post*, 24 November 2011.

Conclusion

The objective of this study is to evaluate the impact of PAD's uncivil action about the Preah Vihear temple. Apart from the immediate effects such as the deterioration of diplomatic relations and the deaths and damage incurred in border clashes, the nationalist campaign had longer-term repercussions which can only be properly understood within the context of Thailand's post-Cold War policy toward its neighbours in general and Cambodia in particular.

In Chapter II, I have shown that the ending of the Cold War and of the war in Cambodia in the late 1980s opened up great opportunities for a new era of economic development and cooperation in Southeast Asia. Former foes became allies and partners in both political and economic cooperation. Various cross-border schemes were launched to promote growth, spread prosperity, and build friendship among the region's states in order to compete with growing regionalism in other parts of the world. Since the government of Chatichai Choonhavan (1988–91), Thailand has positioned herself as a leader and centre of economic cooperation in the region. In the eyes of Thai policy-makers, Cambodia, Laos and Vietnam were no longer enemies, but potential partners in many schemes of bilateral and multilateral cooperation.

Cambodia became an increasingly important country for Thai exports and investment. Both countries benefited from growing trans-border economic activities. Relations between the countries reflected this growing interdependence. In other words, policies promoted by various state agencies reshaped the fundamental fact of the relationship between Thailand and Cambodia from enmity to economic interdependence. Thailand could no longer employ economic measure, such as border closure, to punish its neighbour as it had done during the Cold War. Even when the diplomatic relationship between the governments of Abhisit and Hun Sen slid downhill and several bloody border clashes took place, both sides were careful not to let trans-border business be disrupted. Although Abhisit announced he would suspend financial aid to Cambodia and revoke the maritime MOU, he quietly failed to act on his promise since Thailand would suffer in the long term. While political leaders often act for short-term reasons such as winning approval from a public stirred up by nationalist sentiment, state agencies involved in making foreign policy over the long term are bound to take a more strategic view; they understood that Thailand's growing trans-border economic empire did not give Thailand any edge over Cambodia, but rather made the two countries more and more interdependent.

In Chapter III, I showed that Thai-Cambodian cooperation on the Preah Vihear temple was located within the framework of Thailand's strategy to become a regional economic centre and leader. Although the public tends to see the temple issue as a dispute over territorial sovereignty, in fact Thailand's cooperation with Cambodia over the project to list the temple as a World Heritage site arose from Thailand's cross-border tourism strategy, which later became a significant part of regional integration policy within the frameworks of GMS and ACMECS.

The Thai public has also been impressed by PAD's allegation that Thai policy on the temple was somehow linked to Thaksin's business deals in Cambodia. But this perception overlooks the fact that the policy was pursued consistently by three governments, including the government of General Surayud Julanond which was installed after an anti-Thaksin coup. People who are familiar with the foreign policy process would know that various bureaucratic agencies are involved in interstate issues. As governments tend to change quite frequently in Thailand, bureaucrats are key to making policy continuous and consistent. The Foreign Ministry, Royal Survey Department, army, and National Security Council were all involved in shaping policy over the temple. Although they were committed to defending Thailand's claims to sovereignty over the disputed area, they also wished to promote cross-border cooperation and to strengthen friendship with Cambodia. The cooperation over the temple began in an attempt to turn the once disputed monument into a symbol of friendship and cooperation between the two countries. For the first time in Southeast Asia two formerly antagonistic states were employing cultural methods to settle a territorial dispute. The policies crafted by these state agencies was not overshadowed by the history of "lost territories" which the nationalists wished to revive. Though the bilateral efforts to settle the highly sensitive issue of territorial sovereignty faced many hurdles along the way, both sides showed goodwill, flexibility, and sensitivity toward each other. They were moving toward a peaceful solution which would have been historic and praiseworthy.

The ultra-nationalist movement launched by PAD derailed this essay in cooperation. In Chapter IV, I have shown that the irrational demands and violent actions of the nationalists badly tarnished Thailand's international image. A country cannot become a regional leader without building trust and respect among its neighbours. The PAD campaign worked directly against Thailand's post-Cold War strategy in the region. Instead of becoming a symbol of friendship, the temple became a symbol of hatred between Thailand and Cambodia. Undoing this damage will take a long time.

The success of PAD's campaign to derail the temple listing was partly due to its manipulation of royal-nationalist history regarding the lost territories. The 1962 ICJ decision on Preah Vihear temple is now part of that history. The success also has to be attributed to the support which PAD enjoyed from various civic groups and institutions. Their support helped to legitimize PAD's propaganda, which has now dominated public misperception of the issue. The fixation with getting rid of Thaksin and his proxies meant that little attention was paid to the impact of the nationalist campaign on Thailand's international standing and relations with neighbouring countries. The PAD campaign not only polarized Thai society but pushed the country to the verge of a war with Cambodia.

Although PAD leaders claimed to act within a framework of democracy, in truth their actions tended towards a middle-class based authoritarianism. They exploited popular ignorance about history, regional relations, and economic realities to generate an aggressive nationalism directed against a neighbour. The role of PAD challenges the conventional wisdom that active civil society movements contribute to democratization. While supposedly conservative state agencies in Thailand and Cambodia were working towards a peaceful and sustainable solution, the civil society campaign aggravated hatred and distrust between the peoples of the two countries. The post-

Cold War relationship between Thailand and her neighbours was revealed as fragile and vulnerable, despite the efforts at cooperation. The power of nationalism and historical antagonism triumphed over government efforts to build good neighbourliness.

A civil society movement that strays from democratic principles cannot be expected to have a positive impact on foreign relations. PAD's campaign encouraged a sense of superiority and prejudice toward smaller neighbours, and a lack of respect for international norms and laws as shown by its rejection of the 1962 verdict and its demands for the Thai government to use force against Cambodia. An active civil society movement is not necessarily good for foreign relations. One needs to scrutinize its ideologies, demands, actions, and objectives before one can judge whether a movement is democratic and constructive with respect to regional integration.

Last but not least, another implication of this story is that the future study of foreign relations in Southeast Asia needs to take account of the growing influence of civil society movements in many countries in the region. A deep-rooted, anti-neighbour nationalism is found not only in Thailand but is also rather common among people in the region. In the past, only state agencies exploited nationalism for their hidden agendas. But nationalism is no longer a state monopoly. It can be manipulated by non-state actors against government and its foreign policy. This shared aspect of Southeast Asian societies must be taken seriously if ASEAN wishes to achieve a true sense of community.

Bibliography

Literature in English

Anek Laothamatas, ed. *Democratization in Southeast and East Asia*. Singapore: Institute of Southeast Asian Studies, 1997.

ACMECS. "ACMECS Projects". <http://www.acmecs.org/index.php?id=124> (accessed 20 May 2006).

Asian Development Bank. *Technical Assistance to the Mekong/Lancang River Tourism Planning Study*. June 1997. <www.adb.org/Documents/TARs/REG/30015-STU-TAR.pdf> (accessed 6 January 2011).

Beittinger-Lee, Verena. *(Un)Civil Society and Political Change in Indonesia*. London and New York: Routledge, 2010.

Cohen, Jean L. and Andrew Arato. *Civil Society and Political Theory*. Cambridge: MIT Press, 1992.

Conners, Michael K. and Kevin Hewison. "Introduction: Thailand and the "Good Coup". *Journal of Contemporary Asia* 38, no. 1 (February 2008): 1–10.

Diamond, Larry J. "Toward Democratic Consolidation". *Journal of Democracy* 5, no. 3 (July 1994): 4–17.

Dosch, Jorn. *Changing Dynamics of Southeast Asian Politics*. Boulder: Lynne Rienner, 2007.

Foley, Michael and Bob Edwards. "The Paradox of Civil Society". *Journal of Democracy* 7, no. 3 (1996): 38-52.

International Chamber of Commerce, the United Nations. *An Investment Guide to Cambodia: Opportunities and Conditions*. Geneva, 2004. <http://unctad.org/en/docs/iteiia20036_en.pdf> (accessed 10 August 2010).

International Crisis Group. *Waging Peace: ASEAN and the Thai-Cambodian Border Conflict*. Asia Report No. 215, 6 December 2011.

International Court of Justice. *Reports of Judgments, Advisory Opinions and Orders, Case Concerning the Temple of Preah Vihear (Cambodia v. Thailand), Judgment of 15 June 1962*.

International Court of Justice. "Request for interpretation of the judgment of 15 June 1962 in the case concerning the Temple of Preah Vihear (Cambodia v. Thailand) and Request for the Indication of Provisional Measures". 18 July 2011 <http://www.icj-cij.org/docket/files/151/16564.pdf> (accessed 1 August 2011).

Joint Communiqué between Thailand and Cambodia. 18 June 2008.

Kitirianglarp, Kengkij and Kevin Hewison. "Social Movements and Political Opposition in Contemporary Thailand". *The Pacific Review* 22, no. 4 (2008): 451–77.

Kopecký, Petr. 'Civil Society, Uncivil Society and Contentious Politics in Post-Commnist Europe". In *Uncivil Society? Contentious Politics in Post-Communist Europe,* edited by Petr Kopecký and Cas Mudde, pp. 1–18. London and New York: Routledge, 2003.

Kopecký, Petr and Cas Mudde, eds. *Uncivil Society? Contentious Politics in Post-Communist Europe.* London and New York: Routledge, 2003.

Lim Vatha. "Petroleum Company and Management Project, Cambodia Case Study Update on Petroleum Activities in Cambodia". February 2006 <http://www.ccop.or.th/ppm/document/CAWS6/CAWS6DOC04_vatha.pdf> (accessed 30 August 2008).

Ministry of Tourism, Cambodia. *Tourism Statistical Report 2008.* Phnom Penh, n.d., <http://www.tourismcambodia.com/ftp/Cambodia_Tourism_Statistics_2008.pdf> (accessed 6 January 2011).

Ministry of Foreign Affairs, Thailand. *The Foreign Ministry's Works Between 1997–2000.* Bangkok: n.d.

———. "The Kingdom of Cambodia". <www.mfa.go.th/web/479.php?id=51> (accessed 10 May 2006).

Ministry of Trade and Industry Singapore. "Mr Lim Hng Kiang at the Luncheon with Singapore Business Community in Honour of Samdech Akka Moha Sena Padei Techo Hun Sen PM of the Kingdom of Cambodia, 26 July 2010". <http://app.mti.gov.sg/default.asp?id=148&articleID=22482> (accessed on 6 April 2012).

Mudde, Cas. "Civil society in post-communist Europe: Lessons from the 'dark side'". in *Uncivil Society? Contentious Politics in Post-Communist Europe,* edited by Petr Kopecký and Cas Mudde, pp. 157–70. London and New York: Routledge, 2003.

O'Donnell, Guillermo and Phillip C. Schmitter. *Transitions from Authoritarian Rule: Tentative Conclusions about Uncertain Democracies.* Baltimore: Johns Hopkins University Press, 1986.

Office of Archaeology, Fine Arts Department, Ministry of Culture and ICOMOS, Thailand. *Management Plan for Preah Vihear Mountain and Its Setting.* Bangkok, 2008.

Office of the Council of Ministers, Cambodia. *The Temple of Preah Vihear Inscribed on the World Heritage List (UNESCO) since 2008.* Phnom Penh, 2010.

———. "Summary of the Results of the 34th Session of the World Heritage Committee". 2 August 2010 <//ki-media.blogspot.com/2010/08/summary-of-results-of-34th-session-of.html> (accessed 30 August 2010).

————. "Clarification No. 007/PRU/2010 dated February 12, 2010". <www.pressocm. gov.kh/PRESS-RELEASE/PR2010/CLA_11022010_ENG.pdf> (accessed 13 January 2010).

Pavin Chachawalpongpun. "Confusing Democracies: Diagnosing Thailand's Democratic Crisis, 2001–8". In *Political Change, Democratic Transitions, and Security in Southeast Asia*, edited by Mely Cabellero-Anthony, pp. 34–52. New York: Routledge, 2010.

————. "Diplomacy under Siege Thailand's Political Crisis and the Impact on Foreign Policy". *Contemporary Southeast Asia* 31, no. 3 (2009): 447–67.

————. "Embedding Embittered History: Unending Conflicts in Thai-Cambodian Relations". *Asian Affairs* XLII, no. 1 (March 2012): 81–102.

Puangthong Rungswasdisab. "Thailand's Response to the Cambodian Genocide". In *Genocide in Cambodia and Rwanda: New Perspectives*, edited by Sue Cook, pp. 73–118. New Brunswick: Transaction, 2006.

Pye, Oliver and Wolfram Schaffar. "The 2006 Anti-Thaksin Movement in Thailand: An Analysis". *Journal of Contemporary Asia* 38, no. 1 (February 2008): 38–61.

Putnam, Robert D. "Bowling Alone: America's Declining Social Capital". *Journal of Democracy* 6 (January 1995): 65–78.

Thailand Board of Investment. "Trade and Investment in Cambodia". <www.boi. go.th/thai/clma/2009_cambodia_d5_5-1html> (accessed on 24 July 2009).

The National Committee for the World Heritage. "Statement dated September 3, 2010". www.pressocm.gov.kh/PRESS-RELEASE/PR2010/ST03092010_EN_ 01.pdf (accessed 13 January 2011).

Thompson, Mark R. "People Power Sours: Uncivil Society in Thailand and the Philippines". *Current History* (November 2008): 381–87.

Thongchai Winichakul. *Siam Mapped: A History of the Geo-body of a Nation*. Honolulu: University of Hawaii Press, 1994.

————. "Toppling Democracy". *Journal of Contemporary Asia* 38, no. 1 (February 2008): 11–37.

University of Thai Chamber of Commerce. *Study on Investment Promotion in Laos, Cambodia, and Myanmar*. Bangkok: 2004.

Vannarith, Chheng. *Cambodia: Between China and Japan*. Working Paper no. 31. Cambodian Institute of Cooperation and Peace, 2009. <http://www.cicp.org. kh/download/CICP%20Working%20series/CICP%20Working%20Paper%20N o%2031_Cambodia_Between%20China%20and%20Japan%20by%20Cheang%2 0Vannarith.pdf> (accessed 20 October 2011).

Walker, Andrew. "Phra Viharn: The Dividing Line in Thailand". *New Mandala*, August 2008 <http://asiapacific.anu.edu.au/newmandala/2008/08/25/phra-viharn-the-dividing-line-in-thailand/ > (accessed 5 December 2010).

World Heritage Committee. *The 31ˢᵗ Session of the Committee — Christchurch, New Zealand — July 2007. Decision No 31 COM 8B.24.*

Woldring, Henk E. S. "State and Civil Society in the Political Philosophy of Alexis de Tocqueville". *Voluntas* 9, no. 4 (1998): 363–73.

Yoshifumi, Tamada. *Myth and Realities: The Democratization of Thai Politics.* Kyoto: Kyoto University Press, 2008.

Literature in Thai

Bavornsak Uwanno. *Chae ekkasanlap thi sut prasat phrawihan pho.so.2505-2551* [Disclosing the highly confidential documents, the Temple of Preah Vihear 1962–2008]. Bangkok: Matichon Publications, 2008.

Charnvit Kasetsiri. *Latthi chatniyom thai/sayam kap kamphucha: lae korani suksa prasart khaophrawihan* [Siamese/Thai nationalism and Cambodia: A case study of the Preah Vihear Temple]. Bangkok: Foundation of the Promotion of the Social Science and Humanities Book Project, 2009.

———. *Pramuan sonthisanya anusanya khwamtoklong bantuekkhwamkhaochai lae phanthi rawang sayam prathetthai kap prathet asian phuenban: kamphucha-lao-phama-malaysia* [Collected Treaties-Conventions-Agreements-Memorandum of Understanding and Maps, Between Siam/Thailand-Cambodia-Laos-Burma-Malaysia]. Bangkok: The Social Science and Humanity Textbook Project, 2011.

Duangthida Rames. *Prasat phrawihan kap buengna buenglang praden khatyaeng thai-kamphucha* [The Preah Vihear Temple and the Making of the Thai-Cambodian Conflict]. Bangkok: Katha, n.d.

"Kantopto kamphucha: miti thangkotmai lae kantangprathet" [Response to Cambodia: the legal and foreign policy aspects]. Paper for a public seminar forum organized by Faculty of Law, Chulalongkorn University on 16 November 2009.

Manager Editorial Board. *Prasart phrawihan khwamching thi khonthai tongru* [The Preah Vihear Temple: The Truth Thai People Must Know]. Bangkok: Baan Phra Athit Publication, 2008.

Ministry of Foreign Affairs, Thailand. *Korani karnkhun thabian prasart phraviharn pen moradoklok* [The Inscription of the Temple of Preah Vihear on the World Heritage List]. Bangkok, June 2008.

Morakot Jaewjinca Meyer and Akkarapong Khamkhoon. *Khetdaen farangset-nethoeland-maenam danub* [Boundaries of France-The Netherlands and the Danube River]. Bangkok: The Social Science and Humanity Textbooks Project, 2011.

Office of the National Economic and Social Development Board. *Phaenyuttasat phuea rongrab khrongkan pattana khwamruammue thang settakit nai anuphumiphak maenamkhong hok pratet (thai wiatnam lao kamphucha phama lae monthonyunnan)*

[Strategic Plan to Facilitating the Economic Cooperation Development Project in the Six-country Mekong River Basin Sub-region (Thailand, Vietnam, Laos, Cambodia, Myanmar and Yunnan Province]. Bangkok, 1995, pp. 6–21.

———. *Progress and Direction for Developing Special Economic Zone and Economic Corridor to Neighbouring Countries*. Bangkok, 2001.

Panat Tassaneeyanont, Prasit Piwawatthanapanich, and Wiphol Kitithasanasonchai. *Sanlok-sananuyatotulakan kapkhophiphatrawangprathet* [International Court of Justice-Permanent Court of Arbitration]. Bangkok: The Social Science and Humanity Textbooks Project, 2011.

Pichet Saiphan and Suriya Khamwaan. *Khetdaen viatnam-chin-kamphucha-lao* [*Boundaries of Vietnam-China-Cambodia*-Laos]. Bangkok: The Social Science and Humanity Textbook Project, 2011.

Puangthong Pawakapan and Ronnaphol Masantisuk. *Khetdaenchin-rutsia-mongkolia* [Boundaries of China-Russia and Mongolia]. Bangkok: The Social Science and Humanity Textbook Project, 2011.

Puangthong Pawakapan. *Songkhram kankha lae chatniyom nai khwamsamphan thai-kamphucha* [Wars, Trade and Nationalism in Thai-Cambodian Relations]. Bangkok: The Foundation of the Textbooks Project, 2009.

Onanong Thippimon, Thanasak Saichampa, Dulayaphak Preecharat, Supalak Kanchanakhundee, and Akkarapong Khamkhoon, *Khetdaen sayam/thai-malesia-phama-lao-kamphucha* [Boundaries of Siam/Thailand-Malaysia-Burma-Laos-Cambodia]. Bangkok: The Social Science and Humanity Textbook Project, 2011.

Srisak Vallibhodom. *Khaophraviharn rabert wela ananikhom* [The Preah Vihear Temple: A Time-bomb from Colonialism]. Bangkok: Matichon Publication, 2008.

Suwit Theerasatwat. *Bueangluek kansia dindaeng lae panha prasat phrawihan chak ro.so.112 tueng patchuban* [Insight to the territory losses and the problem of the Preah Vihear Temple from 1893 to the present]. Bangkok: History Association, 2010.

Thailand Institute of Scientific and Technological Research, *Krongkarn chadtham phaenpatibatkarn phattana samliem thongthiew chuemyong thai lao kamphucha* [Operational Plan for Developing the Triangular Tourism among Thailand, Laos, and Cambodia]. Bangkok: Report submitted to Tourism Authority of Thailand, 1999.

Thamrongsak Petchlert-anan. *Sayam thai kap dindaen nai kamphucha lae lao* [Siam-Thailand and "Territories" in Cambodia and Laos]. Bangkok: The Foundation of the Textbooks Project, 2009.

The Sub-committee for Enhancing Thailand's Competitiveness (SECT). *Samut pokkhao kanphoemkit khwamsamat nai kankhaengkhan kap tangprathet* [The white paper report on enhancing Thailand's international competitiveness]. Bangkok, 1995.

Thongchai Winichakul. "Prawattisat thai baep rachachatniyom: chak yuk ananikhom amphrang su rachachatniyom mai rue latthi sadet pho khong kradumphi thai nai patchuban" [The Thai royal nationalist history: From the era of crypto-colonialism to the new royal nationalism, or the contemporary Rama V Cult of Thai Bourgeoisie] *Silapa Watthanatham* 22, no. 1 (November 2001): 55–65.

Watcharin Yongsiri. *Kankha chaidaenthai kap kamphucha panha thi prasop nai patchuban lae naeothang kaekhai* [Border Trade between Thailand and Cambodia: Problems and Solutions]. Bangkok: Asian Studies Institute, Chulalongkorn University, 2004.

Watcharin Yongsiri et al. *Kankha thai-indochin* [Trade between Thailand and Indochina]. Bangkok: Asian Studies Institute, Chulalongkorn University, 1992.

Newspapers

"Abhisit and PAD at loggerhead over the temple issue". *Bangkok Post*, 8 August 2010.

"Abhisit rejects Hun Sen's ceasefire plan". *Bangkok Post*, 18 February 2011.

"Abhisit's govt needs to redefine the national interest". *Bangkok Post*, 19 November 2009.

"Adul chaesam khetkanchon prawihan siang ruk dindaenthai" [Adul exposes the Preah Vihear Temple's buffer zone risks violating Thai territory]. *ASTV Manager Online*, 18 July 2008 <www.manager.co.th/Politics/ViewNews.aspx?NewsID=9510000084451> (accessed 20 July 2008).

"Akkarapong khamkhoon chaeng huachai maichai khmen" [Akkarapong Khamkhoon cries my heart is not Khmer]. *Krungthep Turakij*, 3 March 2011.

"Arrested Thais were on Cambodian territory: Kasit". *The Nation*, 1 January 2011.

"ASEAN mission welcome to monitor Thai-Cambodian border, Kasit says". *The Nation*, 24 February 2011.

"Bueangluek patibatkan hakkhamen lomphaenchatkan phrawihan" [Insight to an operation to topple Cambodia's management plan for the Temple of Preah Vihear]. *Matichon*, 31 July 2010 <http://www.matichon.co.th/play_clip.php?newsid=1280528257> (accessed 31 July 2010).

"An tem tem khamsamphat khong hun sen lae kantopto chak krasuangkantangprathet khong thai" [Read in full, Hun Sen's interview and the response from the Thai Foreign Ministry]. *Prachatai*, 11 November 2009 <http://prachatai.com/journal/2009/11/26539> (accessed 11 November 2009).

"Cabinet revokes MOU on maritime border". *Bangkok Post*, 11 November 2009.

"Cambodia, Malaysia pledge to further trade, investment relations". *People's Daily Online*, 12 May 2010. <http://english.people.com.cn/90001/90778/90858/90863/6982055.html> (accessed on 16 April 2012).

"Cambodia B1.4bn loan still on". *Bangkok Post*, 29 November 2009.

"Cambodia files an Application requesting interpretation of the Judgment rendered by the Court on 15 June 1962 in the case concerning the Temple of Preah Vihear (Cambodia v. Thailand) and also asks for the urgent indication of provisional measures". Press release, ICJ, 2 May 2011.

"Cambodian PM Hun Sen: Thailand must honour the Court decision; Indonesian observers are a must". *Nokorwat News Daily*, 27 July 2011 <http://nokorwatnews.com/detailnews.php?newsid=12920&mnu=2&cid=4> (accessed 10 April 2012).

"Cancel other pacts, financial aid projects to Cambodia, PAD urges". *Bangkok Post*, 8 November 2009.

Chamnan Chanrueng. "Kanchai amnattulakan an pen issara kapkankrathamphit to tamnaengnathi nai kanyuttitham" [The exercise of independent judicial power and the abuse of judicial power]. *Prachatai*, 9 March 2001 <http://prachatai.com/journal/2011/03/33456> (accessed 9 March 2001).

"Che pong hoem paksia prachot chuan phanthamit klapban noichai khao phrathep borichak khathanai 4 kharatchakan thuek phanthamit fong" [Anchalee bad mouthing, upset news of Princess Sirindhon donates money to help four bureaucrats accused by the PAD]. *Thai Insider*, 3 October 2008 <//thaienews.blogspot.com/2008/10/4_6567.html> (accessed 10 October 2008).

"Chichata thai sia dindaen? Chuad sappayakon mahasan hak unesco rap phaen khmen" [Thai will lose enormous natural resources if UNESCO accepted Cambodia's plan]. *Thairath*, 29 July 2010.

"Court orders revocation of Preah Vihear joint communiqué". *Bangkok Post*, 29 December 2008.

Daniel Ten Kate and Anuchit Nguyen. "Thailand to Comply with Cambodian Temple DMZ Imposed by UN". *Bloomberg*, 18 July 2011 <http://www.bloomberg.com/news/2011-07-18/thailand-to-comply-with-cambodian-temple-dmz-imposed-by-un.html> (accessed 10 April 2012).

"Diplomacy set to pay dividend in Cambodia". *Bangkok Post*, 6 September 2010.

"Diplomacy the new battlefront". *The Nation*, 8 February 2011.

"Editorial". *Khom Chad Luek*, 13 November 2009.

"Editorial". *Matichon*, 14 November 2009.

"Govt and PAD arm reach temple accord". *Bangkok Post*, 9 August 2010.

"Govt plans special economic zone". *Bangkok Post*, 30 August 2010.

"Govt pushes new border checkpoints". *Bangkok Post*, 28 September 2010.

"Govt renew Preah Vihear push". *Bangkok Post*, 18 June 2009.

"Govt spurns help from the UN". *Bangkok Post*, 9 February 2011.

"Had PAD lost its conscience?". *Bangkok Post*, 9 February 2011.

"Hun Sen, Abhisit start summit war of words". *Bangkok Post*, 24 October 2009.

"Hun Sen blames Thailand (and Abhisit) all the way". *Bangkok Post*, 12 November 2010.

"Hun Sen krao mee rueang kap mak doitrong" [Hun Sen toughens, having problem with Abhisit only]. *Matichon*, 11 November 2009.

"Hun Sen ngamna haisampathan namman khetthapson ao thai" [The shameless Hun Sen grants oil concession in the overlapping claimed area off the Gulf of Thailand]. *ASTV Manager Online*, 23 July 2009 <www.manager.co.th/IndoChina/ViewNews.aspx?NewsID=9520000083341> (accessed 1 December 2010).

"Hun Sen rules out helping with pardon". *Bangkok Post*, 18 February 2011.

"Hun Sen-Thaksin yam thai khao khmen tiw kunsue" [Hun Sen-Thaksin insult Thailand! Enter Cambodia to coach the mastermind]. *Khom Chud Luek*, 9 November 2009.

"Kankha trat phang lang thai riak thut klap chak khmen" [The border trade at Trad suffers after Thailand recalls the ambassador]. *Matichon*, 5 November 2009.

Khammakan moradoklok luean phicharana khuenthabian phrawihan pina" [The World Heritage Committee postpones the inscription of the Phreah Vihear Temple to next year]. *Matichon*, 30 June 2009.

"Kham to kham sondhi chi loek m.o.u. 43 kon sia 1.5 lan rai hai khmen" [Work by word, Sondhi urges to revoke MOU 2000 before losing 1.5 million rai to Cambodia]. *ASTV Manager Online*, 24 July 2010 <http://www.manager.co.th/politics/ViewNews.aspx?NewsID=9530000102053> (accessed on 4 December 2010).

"Kankaekhai panha khaophrawihan baep sonthi limthongkun" [Solving the problem of the Temple of Preah Vihear in Sondhi Limthongkul's style]. *Prachatai*, 28 July 2008 <http://prachatai.com/journal/2008/07/17535> (accessed 8 October 2008).

"Khaew rattaban mee mue nung kae panhakhamen" [Mocking, the government has the best hand to solve problem with Cambodia]. *Matichon*, 2 December 2009.

"Kham to kham aphisit aphiprai korani prasat phra vihan" [Abhisit's parliamentary debate]. <www.praviharn.net/images/stories/apisit_word_to_word.pdf> (accessed 1 October 2010).

"Klangchat rue rakchat? Botrian chak prasat phrawihan" [Chauvinism or Patriotism? a lesson from the Preah Vihear Temple]. *Krungthep Turakij*, 7 March 2011.

"Ko kong sunklang ratthaksin thalom thai" [Koh Kong, center of the Thaksin State to attack Thailand]. *Kom Chad Luek*, 13 November 2009.

"Kongthap guarantee mai siadindaen khunthabian khaophrawihan moradoklok" [The army guarantees the Temple listing will cause no territorial loss]. *Thairath*, 19 June 2008.

"Mark ngat sonthisanya la no.cho.maew leng yokradap to khmen hak duephang" [Mark (Abhisit) employs treaty to hunt for the convicted Thaksin, aims to toughen measure against Cambodia if recalcitrant]. *ASTV Manager Online*, 10 September 2009 <http://www.manager.co.th/Politics/ViewNews.aspx?NewsID=9520000135334> (accessed 10 Septerber 2009).

Mass Communication of Thailand (MCOT). "Thai PM says delayed Preah Vihear temple World Heritage Site registration could solve problems". *English News*, 30 June 2009. <enews.mcot.net/view/php?id=10571> (accessed 30 June 2009).

Mass Communication of Thailand (MCOT). "Four soldiers killed in latest Thai-Cambodian border skirmish". *English News*, <http://enews.mcot.net/view.php?id=9339> (accessed 10 January 2011).

Michael Hayes. "The View from Cambodia". *Phnom Penh Post*, 17 February 2011.

"Mong anakot khao phrawihan…thai tongruthan maisia kha ngo" [Gazing at the future of the Preah Vihear Temple…Thais must not be fooled]. *ASTV Manager Online*, 4 July 2008 <http://www.manager.co.th/Travel/ViewNews.aspx?NewsID=9510000082791> (accessed 30 July 2008).

"Mo.tho.pho.2 at khonbangklum mi khwamkityai sangpanha mairuchop" [The Second Regional Army chief slams the politically ambitious group, creating never ending problems]. *Matichon*, 31 December 2010.

"Mo.tho. sho nganwichai 24 withi thi ratthaban thaksin saeksaeng sue" [TU's research reveals Thaksin's 24 methods of interfering with media]. *Prachatai*, 14 November 2008, <http://www.prachatai.com/journal/2008/11/18937> (accessed 24 November 2008).

"Nakwichakan ting luek m.o.u. thai sia- lai chat chong suam prayot naikhamen" [Academic warns Thailand would lose if MOU invoked — many countries wait to take over advantages in Cambodia]. *Krunthep Turkij*, 22 November 2009.

"Navy chief warns govt on MOU". *Bangkok Post*, 21 November 2009.

"Neighbours recommended for heavy-industry projects". *Bangkok Post*, 18 August 2010.

"No plan to sell PTT: Kittirat". *The Nation*, 10 February 2012.

"Noppadol top kratu so.wo. o penphucheracha maihai thai siang siadindaen" [Noppadol responses to senators, claims to prevent Thailand from territorial loss]. *Matichon*, 19 June 2008.

"Our Boundaries, Our Neighbors". Documentary film by the Social Science and Humanity Textbooks Project, 2011 <http://textbooksproject.org/?page_id=821> and <http://www.youtube.com/watch?v=W7gqf3WwcwM>.

"Phakonkong khmen hup khao phrawihan" [Exposing Cambodia's cheating to take over the Preah Vihear Temple], *ASTV Manager Online*, 30 September 2009 <www.manager.co.th/QOL/ViewNews.aspx?NewsID=9520000114481> (accessed 14 January 2011 "Road funds for Cambodia unfrozen," *Bangkok Post*, 27 August 2010.

"Phanthamit chi abhisit leo kwa thaksin 3 thao" [PAD says Abhisit is three times worse than Thaksin], *Prachatai*, 10 March 2011 <http://prachatai.com/journal/2011/03/33468> (accessed 10 March 2011).

"Pho.bo.tho.bo. lan khrai yakrop choenma thi phrawihan"[Army Chief says anyone want to fight, please come to the Preah Vihear Temple". *Matichon*, 4 February 2011.

"PM, all seven ministers survive censure debate". *Bangkok Post*, 27 June 2008.

"PM rejects land loss claims". *Bangkok Post*, 5 July 2010.

"PM thanks rally, blames Noppadon". *Bangkok Post*, 1 August 2010.

"PM urges Unesco to end chaos". *Bangkok Post*, 11 February 2011.

"Po.cho.po. khan phanthamit sanoe thontua chak phaki moradoklok" [Democrat opposes PAD's call to withdraw from the World Heritage Committee], *ASTV Manager Online*, 4 December 2010 <www.manager.co.th/Politics/ViewNews.aspx?NewsID=9530000171204> (accessed 20 December 2010).

"Pongpol: Temple's listing irreversible". *Bangkok Post*, 1 July 2009.

"Prakat luanglok chak bantuek m.o.u. 2544 tueng moradoklok" [The deceptive announcement, from the 2001 MOU to the world heritage]. *Matichon*, 5 September 2011 <http://www.matichon.co.th/news_detail.php?newsid=1315192414&grp id=01&catid&subcatid> (accessed 5 September 2011).

PTT Exploration and Production Public Com Ltd. "PTTEP Participation in Petroleum Block B, Cambodia". April 2005 <http://www.pttep.com/en/newsDetail.aspx?ContentID=45 > (accessed 28 February 2011).

Puangthong Pawakapan, "Prasat khaophrawihan, m.o.u.2543, lae phaenthi" [The Preah Vihear Temple, MOU 2000, and Map], *Matichon*, 3 August 2010.

"Road funds for Cambodia unfrozen". *Bangkok Post*, 28 August 2010.

"Ruk poed wethi khaophrawihan tan sanlok tan thonthahan-ham Indonesia chun" [Move to open the Preah Vihear Temple forum, oppose World Court, oppose troop withdrawal, bar Indonesia's interference], *ASTV Manager Online*, 4 March 2012 <http://www.manager.co.th/South/ViewNews.aspx?NewsID=95500000 28766> (accessed 10 April 2012).

"Samak jibes at temple injunction". *Bangkok Post*, 7 August 2008.

"Samphan luek-phonprayot longtua prasatphrawihan-thaksin-al fayet-po.to.tho" [Deep relationship-consensual benefit-Thaksin-Al Fayet-PTT], *ASTV Manager Online*, 22 July 2008 <http://www.manager.co.th/Daily/ViewNews.aspx?Ne wsID=9510000085750> (accessed 23 July 2008).

"Sap thalaengkanruam thai-khmen wiparit chae phonprayotthapson maew-hun sen uea" [Trashing the vicious Thai-Cambodian Joint Communiqué, Uncovering Thaksin's and Hun Sen's enormous conflict of interests], *ASTV Manager Online*, 1 July 2008 <www.manager.co.th/Politics/ViewNews.aspx?NewsID=95100000 77227> (accessed 29 July 2008).

"Samphat phiset saneh chammarik" [Special interview with Saneh Chammarik] *Prachatai*, 14 December 2006 <http://prachatai3.info/m/journal/11064> (accessed 26 December 2006).

"Sewana prasat phrawihan kangkha mi khon yubueanglang yuyaeng" [Seminar on the Temple of Preah Vihear, doubt somebody is behind the scene to incite problem], *Matichon*, 30 June 2008.

"Sewana hua ok khonthai lae thurakitthai nai kampucha" [Seminar on the faith of Thai people and business in Cambodia". *Prachatai*, 12 November 2009 <www.prachatai.com/journal/2009/11/26555> (accessed 13 November 2009).

"Sondhi at mark yatuang thanon 2 len lai hai pai thuang 4.6 to.ro.ko.mo." [Sondhi attacks Abhisit, don't reclaim the 2 len-road, go reclaim the 4.6 sq.km], *Prachatai*, 11 February 2011 <http://prachatai.com/journal/2011/02/33065> (accessed 11 February 2011).

"Sondhi chuak nakwichakan appayot mark nakprachatippatai chomplom" [Sondhi attacks disgraceful academics — Abhisit the fake Democrat], *Manager Online*, 10 February 2011 <www.manager.co.th/asp-bin/mgrview.aspx?NewsID=9540 000017891> (accessed 10 February 2011).

"Sondhi lai prayuth pai len li-ke pen thahan mai pokpong phaendin" [Sondhi tells Prayuth to be a folk dancer if he does not want to protect the land], *ASTV Manager Online*, 5 February 2011 <www.manager.co.th/Politics/ViewNews.aspx?NewsID=9540000015954> (accessed 5 February 2011).

"Sondhi yu khongthap bukyuet nakhonwat laek prasatphrawihan" [Sondhi urges army to occupy Angkor Wat in exchange for the return of the Preah Vihear Temple], *Prachatai*, 8 February 2011 <http://prachatai.com/journal/2011/02/33005> (accessed 8 February 2011).

Sunan Srichantra. "Ta to ta fun to fun phue daikhuen khaophrawihan" [An eye for an eye, a tooth for a tooth for the return of the Preah Vihear Temple], *Nation Weekly*, 5 October 2009.

"Surapong Jayanama lokkhrap kaeng phontokkimulai" [Surapong Jayanama expose the cockeyed gang], *ASTV Manager Online*, 31 October 2009 <www.thaiday.com/Daily/ViewNews.aspx?NewsID=9520000130300> (accessed 30 October 2010).

Surawit Wirawan. "Prathet khong khon thai chai khmen" [The Nation of Thais with Khmer Hearts], *Manager Online*, 13 January 2011 <http://www.manager.co.th/Daily/ViewNews.aspx?NewsID=9540000004737> (accessed 14 January 14, 2011).

"Tea Banh tueng thai ti golf prawit" [Tea Banh arrives Thailand to play golf with Prawit], *Khom Chud Luek*, 26 November 2009.

"Thai and Cambodia troop clash for fourth day on border". *Reuters*, 7 February 2011 <http://www.reuters.com/article/2011/02/07/us-thailand-cambodia-idUSTRE7151K320110207> (accessed 10 April 2012).

"Thaksin-Hun Sen songkhram namlai thi thuk pokpit, khmen…prathet mi wai khai" [Thaksin-Hun Sen, the disguised war of words, Cambodia..a country for sale?], *Khom Chad Luek*, 11 November 2009.

"Thailand says Indonesian observers not needed in disputed Cambodia border area". *Bangkok Post*, 20 August 2011.

"Thai-kamphucha rop krathop kankha turakit thongthiew donnaksut wan songsinkha wietnam sadut" [Thai-Cambodia battle will affect trade, tourism will be hardest hit, fear export to Vietnam affected] *Matichon*, 9 February 2011.

"Thai troops stand guard near temple". *Bangkok Post*, 1 June 2009.

"Thai troops stay put in the temple area". *Bangkok Post*, 23 November 2011.

The National Human Rights Commission of Thailand, "Open letter from the NHRC, Thailand to Ban Ki-Moon". *Prachatai*, 29 July 2008 <www.prachatai. com/english/node/716> (accessed 29 July 2008).

"Tri-nation highway tour". *Bangkok Post*, 28 August 2010.

Thongchai Winichakul. "Preah Vihear could be a Time Bomb". *The Nation*, 30 June 2008.

"Troops to remain near Preah Vihear". *Bangkok Post*, 24 November 2011.

"UNESCO Director-General regrets the announcement of Thailand's intention to denounce the 1972 World Heritage Convention". 26 June 2011 <http://whc. unesco.org/en/news/772> (accessed 28 June 2011).

"Verdicts hammer govt". *Bangkok Post*, 9 July 2008.

Wanwipa Charoonroj, "Yokluek m.o.u.2544 phro lamoet phantha korani rairaeng" [Revoking the MOU 2001 for it violates the comitment severely] <www. praviharn.net/index.php?option=com_content&view=article&id=130:-mou-2544-new&catid=35:2009-08-01-23-00&itemid+148> (accessed 4 July 2010).

"Wethi panthamit propmuehai thahan thai lang patha khmer" [PAD's rally applauds Thai soldiers after clash with Cambodia], *Prachatai*, 4 February 2011 <http:// prachatai.com/journal/2011/02/32959> (accessed 4 February 2011).

"Worajet yan lakwicha sanpokkhrong maimi khetamnatsan nuea khadi khaophrawihan" [Worajet insists the Administrative Court has no jurisdiction over the Preah Vihear Temple case]. *Prachatai*, 1 July 2008 <http://prachatai. com/journal/2008/07/17229> (accessed 2 July 2008).

"Worajet Phakeerat: san khien rattathammanun mai" [Worajet Pakeerat: Court writes a new constitution]. *Prachatai*, 13 July 2008 <http://prachatai.com/ journal/2008/07/17353> (accessed 17 July 2008).

"WHC postpones decision on temple plan to next year". *Bangkok Post*, 30 July 2010; "Errors stall Cambodian temple bid". *Bangkok Post*, 31 July 2010.

Index

ABOUT THE AUTHOR

Puangthong R. Pawakapan is Associate Professor in the International Relations Department, Chulalongkorn University. Her academic expertise is in the field of Southeast Asian Studies with special interest in the political relationship between Thailand and Cambodia. Political violence is also part of her interest. Puangthong was a Shorenstein APARC/Asia Foundation research fellow for 2010–11 at the Shorenstein Asia Pacific Research Center, Stanford University, where she worked on this book. Between May 1998–July 1999, she was a research affiliate at the Cambodian Genocide Program, Yale University, where she researched on "Thailand's response to the Cambodian Genocide", in *Genocide in Cambodia and Rwanda: New Perspectives* (2004 and 2006). She has a BA in Political Science from Thammasat University, Thailand and a Ph.D. in History from the University of Wollongong in Australia.

www.ingramcontent.com/pod-product-compliance
Lightning Source LLC
Chambersburg PA
CBHW061749270326
41928CB00011B/2433